ag4
MEDIA FACADES

daab

Introduction	4
Different Forms of Programming	12
Interactive Programming	16
CAMPUS | T-Mobile Headquarters | Bonn	22
SCULPTURE | Khalifa Tower | Doha	34
FATA MORGANA | Main Railway Station | Cologne	42
LIFE | Serono Headquarters | Geneva	50
GLOBE | Start Amadeus | Bad Homburg	60
Autoactive Programming	66
WINDOW | Galeria Kaufhof | Alexanderplatz Berlin	72
STADIUM | LTU Arena | Dusseldorf	78
SPIRIT | Media Port | Dusseldorf	84
INSIDE OUT | SRG Television Station | Bern	90
HYPERBOLOID | Nissan Showroom | Doha	96
POP | McDonald's | Chicago	100
Reactive Programming	104
LANDMARK | Congress Centre | Zurich	110
URBAN | International Media Avenue | Beijing	120
GRID | CCTV Broadcasting Station | Beijing	128
THE PEARL | Media environment | Dubai	134
BLOB | Multifunction Arena | Beijing	140
SPEED | Audi Showroom | Munich	146
TIME | Railway Tower in the Sony Center | Berlin	154
ag4 mediatecture company®	160
The media Facade as Part of Urban Culture	166
Index	176

Introduction by Ralf Müller

ag4 mediatecture company® first developed the idea of a transparent media facade as early as 1992. In order to be able to realise this idea and put it into practice, LED technology had to advance to satisfy the special requirements of a media facade. Around the same time there was a rising demand for the number of projects requiring facades to act as communicative interfaces. ag4 thus increasingly faced the challenge of having to motor the development in this direction. However, it was to take eight years until the appropriate ideas could be put into practice and a further four years until the first project of a transparent media facade was realised.

Maintaining transparency while being able to medialise large areas in an economically viable way are parameters which guarantee the success of the transparent media facade. Be it as stainless steel wire mesh or panels – compared to the standard LED screen the transparent media facade is superior in terms of size, cost efficiency and possible fields of application. It does not matter where it is installed – it does not decrease the building's versatility or its utilisation.

Graphics and video, company and brand communication, artistic animations, information and entertainment: the transparent media facade offers manifold possibilities to communicate powerfully and effectively on a large scale. The system of the transparent media facade is always an integral part of the actual building and has to be designed and adapted to each and every project. It is a system with a high degree of individuality and differently configurable resolutions to meet every possible need.

The sensitive dynamisation of buildings on the basis of their individual design and their medialisation has become a reality thanks to the transparent media facade. The projects described in this book provide a retrospect on that which has already been achieved and at the same time serve as an inspiration for the future.

Einleitung von Ralf Müller

Die erste Idee zur Transparenten Medienfassade entstand bei ag4 mediatecture company® bereits 1992. Damit aus der Idee Wirklichkeit werden konnte, musste sich die LED-Technologie noch zugunsten der Anforderungen einer Medienfassade weiterentwickeln.

Zur gleichen Zeit erhöhte sich die Anzahl an Projekten, in denen die Forderung aufgestellt wurde, Gebäudefassaden als kommunikative Schnittstellen nutzbar zu machen. Immer öfter stand ag4 vor der Herausforderung, die Entwicklung in dieser Richtung voran zu treiben. Es dauerte jedoch acht Jahre, bis die entsprechenden Ideen technologisch verwirklicht werden konnten und weitere vier Jahre, bis das erste Projekt einer Transparenten Medienfassade umgesetzt wurde.

Die Erhaltung der Transparenz im Zusammenspiel mit der Möglichkeit, große Flächen auch unter ökonomischen Gesichtspunkten zu medialisieren, sind die Parameter, die den Erfolg der Transparenten Medienfassade ausmachen. Ob als Metallgewebe oder auf Lamellenbasis – die Transparente Medienfassade ist einem geschlossenen LED-Board hinsichtlich Größe, Kosteneffizienz und Einsatzmöglichkeiten überlegen. Dort, wo sie installiert wird, gibt es keine großen Einschränkungen für die Nutzer des Gebäudes.

Grafik und Video, Unternehmens- und Markenkommunikation, künstlerische Animation, Information und Unterhaltung: Die Transparente Medienfassade bietet den Nutzern vielfältige Möglichkeiten, überzeugend in großen Dimensionen mit Nach- und Eindruck zu kommunizieren. Dabei ist das System der Transparenten Medienfassade stets integraler Bestandteil der Architektur und wird jeweils projektspezifisch entworfen. Es ist ein System mit hoher Individualität und unterschiedlich konfigurierbaren Auflösungen, das jedem Kontext gerecht werden kann.

Die sensible Dynamisierung von Gebäuden auf der Grundlage einer individuellen Architektur und ihrer Medialisierung ist durch die Transparente Medienfassade Wirklichkeit geworden. Die in diesem Buch vorgestellten Projekte halten Rückschau auf das Geleistete und geben Anregung und Inspiration für die Zukunft.

Introduction par Ralf Müller

Le premier concept de façade médiatique transparente a été imaginé dès 1992 par ag4 mediatecture company®. Pour pouvoir réaliser cette idée, il fallait cependant développer la technologie DEL de manière à ce qu'elle puisse satisfaire aux exigences d'une façade médiatique. À la même époque, un nombre croissant de projets cherchait un moyen d'exploiter les façades des bâtiments pour en faire des interfaces communicatives. ag4 se vit alors confrontée au défi pressant de développer son concept dans ce sens. Et pourtant, il fallut huit ans pour maîtriser les technologies nécessaires à la réalisation de ces idées, et quatre années supplémentaires avant que le premier projet de façade médiatique transparente ne voie le jour.

Le succès de la façade médiatique transparente repose sur deux paramètres : d'une part, la transparence est conservée, et d'autre part il est possible de médialiser de vastes surfaces, même d'un point de vue économique. Sur toile métallique ou sur lamelles, la façade médiatique transparente offre de nombreux avantages par rapport à un panneau à DEL, notamment en matière de taille, de coût et de possibilités d'exploitation. Les personnes occupant le bâtiment sur lequel la façade est installée ne subissent pas de restrictions importantes.

Images et vidéos, messages d'entreprises et communication de marques, animations artistiques, informations, divertissement : la façade médiatique transparente offre d'innombrables possibilités de communiquer en grand format avec force et effet. Le système de la façade médiatique transparente fait partie intégrante de l'architecture et chaque projet repose sur un concept spécifique. Il s'agit d'un système extrêmement individuel dont les résolutions peuvent être configurées différemment, lui permettent de s'adapter à n'importe quel contexte.

Grâce à la façade médiatique transparente, la dynamisation sensible des bâtiments sur la base d'une architecture individuelle et de sa médialisation est devenue réalité. Les projets présentés dans le présent ouvrage offrent une rétrospective de ce qui a été réalisé et une source de suggestions et d'inspiration pour l'avenir.

Introducción de Ralf Müller

La primera idea de "fachada mediática transparente" surgió en ag4 meadiatecture company® ya en 1992, pero para que pudiera hacerse realidad, fue necesario primero que la tecnología LED se perfeccionase hasta satisfacer las exigencias que una fachada de este tipo exige. En esa época aumentó el número de proyectos que demandaban para las fachadas de los edificios un uso comunicativo de interconexión. ag4 se vio cada vez con más frecuencia ante el reto de llevar la evolución por esos derroteros. Pese a todo, para que el primer proyecto de fachada mediática transparente se llevara a la práctica, aún tuvieron que pasar ocho años.

La conservación de la transparencia unida a la posibilidad de la mediatización de grandes superficies con fines económicos son los parámetros sobre los que se asienta el éxito de las fachadas mediáticas transparentes. Ya sea a modo de estructura metálica o sobre una base de láminas - la fachada mediática transparente aventaja al panel LED cerrado tanto por tamaño como por la eficiencia de los costes y las posibilidades de empleo. Donde se instala, no plantea grandes limitaciones a los usuarios del edificio.

Arte gráfico y vídeo, propaganda empresarial y de marcas, animación artística, información y entretenimiento: la fachada mediática transparente ofrece a los usuarios un sinfín de posibilidades de comunicar en grandes dimensiones de modo convincente, enfático y persuasivo. Además, el sistema de las fachadas mediáticas transparentes es siempre un componente integral de la arquitectura y se diseña en cada caso específicamente para el proyecto. Se trata de una técnica con una gran individualidad y soluciones de configuración variable que puede resultar satisfactoria en cualquier contexto.

Las fachadas mediáticas transparentes han hecho posible una dinamización sensitiva de los edificios fundamentada en una arquitectura individualizada y su mediatización. Los proyectos presentados en este libro ofrecen una retrospectiva de los logros y estímulo e inspiración para el futuro.

Introduzione di Ralf Müller

L'idea di facciata mediatica ha iniziato a prendere corpo in ag4 mediatecture company® nel 1992. Perché dall'idea potesse concretizzarsi una realtà, la tecnologia dei LED doveva ancora svilupparsi in direzione di una vera e propria domanda di facciata mediatica. Allo stesso tempo è aumentato il numero dei progetti in cui emergeva la richiesta di rendere le facciate degli edifici interfacce per la comunicazione. E sempre più spesso ag4 si è trovata di fronte a una sfida, quella di lavorare allo sviluppo in quella direzione. Ci sono voluti otto anni perché quelle idee potessero trovare adeguato sviluppo tecnologico e altri quattro anni perché vedesse la luce il primo progetto di facciata mediatica trasparente.

Tra i parametri che determinano il successo delle facciate mediatiche trasparenti, vi è il mantenimento della trasparenza in abbinamento alla possibilità di medializzare grandi superfici, anche dal punto di vista economico. Realizzata in maglia metallica o con una struttura a lamelle, la facciata mediatica trasparente è uno schermo a LED chiuso di qualità altissima per quanto riguarda dimensioni, contenimento dei costi e possibilità di applicazione. Dove viene installata non si verificano limitazioni apprezzabili per gli utenti dell'edificio.

Grafiche multimediali, comunicazioni specifiche dell'azienda o sul marchio, animazione artistica, informazione e intrattenimento: la facciata mediatica trasparente offre un'ampia gamma di possibilità per la comunicazione di grande impatto. In questo senso, il sistema della facciata mediatica trasparente è concepito come parte integrante dell'architettura e viene studiato in modo personalizzato per ogni progetto. Si tratta di un sistema ad alta individualità e che permette soluzioni configurabili in modo diverso, calcolato per adeguarsi a ogni tipo di contesto.

La dinamizzazione sensibile di edifici sulla base di un'architettura personalizzata e la sua medializzazione diventano realtà con la facciata mediatica trasparente. I progetti raccolti nel libro mostrano ciò che è già stato fatto e allo stesso tempo sono fonte d'ispirazione e di stimolo per il futuro.

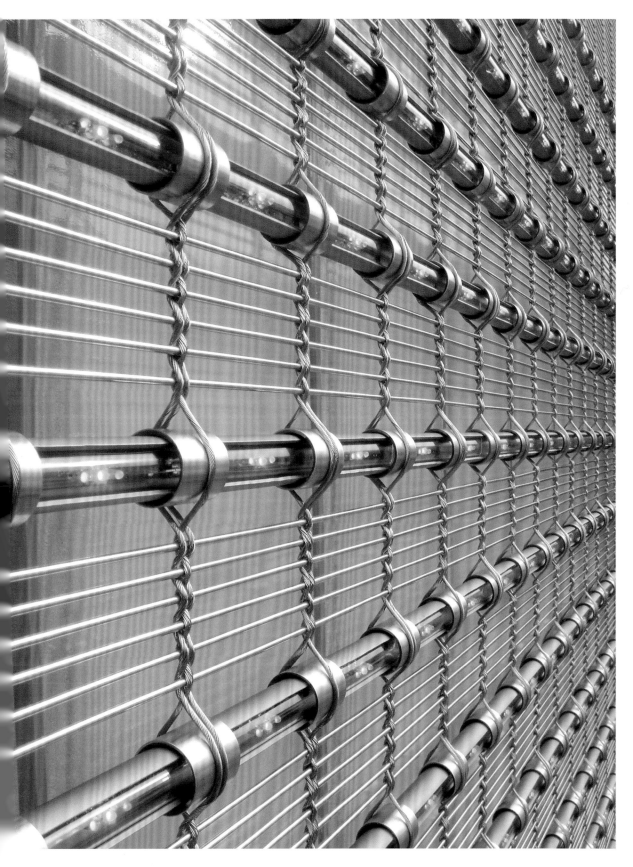

Different Forms of Programming

Due to the satiation of stimuli these days it is very hard to get somebody's attention. Moving images on a dynamic façade have a major advantage when it comes to catching the eye: cognitive psychology dictates that every movement does exactly that by exploiting a natural orientation reflex. Static images, however, disappear with time from the focus of human cognition.

Adequate content of a media facade harmonises with the building's shape and form. Architecture and the medialised display affect one another and are perceived as one – the building appears as a living organism. If the contents and events occurring within the building are medialised on its facade, the building starts to interact with the media programme. This interaction generates a new entity – the interior turns itself inside out and onto the facade.

Classic imagery media such as the cinema or television have a large and ever increasing pool of imagery material at their disposal which has been subject to extensive editorial supervision. Furthermore, the audience can choose which programme to watch. With media facades this is quite different. They are an ever-present item in the urban landscape and thus become an integral part of the people´s space in their everyday lives. They experience the media facade 24 a day all year round. A display of classic advertisements would therefore not do justice to the requirements of a media facade – if only because of the limited pool of imagery material available and its subsequent repetition. The basic parameters of this different cognitive situation demand a new kind of media programme. Over and above the classic imagery and video programmes, digital media offers new possibilities by providing self-generating images, interaction and networking that pay tribute to the altered requirements of media facades. The projects are thus bundled together according to the three different media contents – interactive, autoactive and reactive.

Bespielungsarten

Aufmerksamkeit ist aufgrund der heutigen Reizüberflutung eine knappe Ressource. Bewegte Bilder auf einer dynamischen Fassade haben in dieser Hinsicht einen entscheidenden Vorteil: Wahrnehmungspsychologisch lenkt jede Bewegung, ausgelöst durch einen natürlichen Orientierungsreflex, unsere Aufmerksamkeit auf sich. Statische Bilder hingegen verschwinden mit der Zeit aus dem Fokus menschlicher Wahrnehmung.

Die adäquate Bespielung einer Medienfassade harmoniert mit der Gestalt des Gebäudes. Architektur und präsentierte Bespielungsinhalte beeinflussen sich wechselseitig und werden als ein Ganzes wahrgenommen – das Gebäude tritt als lebendiger Organismus in Erscheinung. Wenn nun die Inhalte und Ereignisse im Gebäude auf der Fassade inszeniert werden, treten Gebäude und Bespielung in Kommunikation. Diese Wechselwirkung generiert eine Einheit – das Innere kehrt sich nach außen auf die Fassade.

Klassische Bildmedien wie Kino oder Fernsehen verfügen sowohl über einen großen, ständig wachsenden Fundus an Bildmaterial mit einer aufwendigen redaktionellen Betreuung als auch über die Möglichkeit der Programmwahl für den Zuschauer. Bei Medienfassaden ist dies anders. Medienfassaden sind durch ihre stationäre Präsenz im Stadtraum für eine große Zahl an Menschen integraler Bestandteil ihres urbanen Alltags. Sie erleben die Medienfassade 24 Stunden am Tag über das ganze Jahr. Eine Bespielung mit klassischen Werbefilmen wird dem Anspruch einer Medienfassade – schon allein wegen der stetigen Wiederholung eines begrenzten Fundus an Bildmaterial – in den meisten Fällen nicht mehr gerecht. Die Rahmenbedingungen dieser veränderten Wahrnehmungssituation verlangen nach neuen Bespielungsarten. Über die klassische Bild- und Filmbespielung hinaus bieten die digitalen Medien hier neue Möglichkeiten durch selbstgenerierende Bilder, Interaktion und Vernetzung, die den veränderten Anforderungen der Bespielung von Medienfassaden gerecht werden. Entsprechend der drei Bespielungsarten – interaktive, autoaktive und reaktive Bespielung – sind die Projekte in diesem Buch drei Kapiteln zugeordnet.

Modes de mises en scène

En raison du matraquage excessif que subit actuellement la population, l'attention est une ressource devenue rare. Des images en mouvement sur une façade dynamique possèdent donc à tous égards un avantage décisif : d'un point de vue psychologique perceptif, notre réflexe naturel d'orientation fait que tout mouvement attire notre attention. Les images statiques, en revanche, finissent par disparaître du foyer de la perception humaine.

Toute mise en scène adéquate d'une façade médiatique doit être en harmonie avec la forme du bâtiment. En effet, l'architecture et les contenus mis en scène s'influencent réciproquement et sont perçus comme un tout. Le bâtiment ressemble alors à un organisme vivant. Si l'on met en scène sur la façade les contenus et les événements qui ont lieu dans le bâtiment, ce dernier entre en communication avec la mise en scène. Cette interaction génère une unité - l'intérieur se tourne vers l'extérieur, sur la façade.

Les médias visuels classiques tels que le cinéma ou la télévision disposent non seulement d'un fonds riche et toujours croissant d'images accompagné d'un suivi rédactionnel précis, mais ils offrent également au spectateur la possibilité de sélectionner les programmes. Sur les façades médiatiques, les choses sont différentes. En raison de leur présence stationnaire en agglomération, les façades médiatiques font, pour un grand nombre de personnes, partie intégrante de la vie urbaine au quotidien. Ils voient cette façade médiatique toute l'année, 24h/24. La diffusion de spots publicitaires classiques - ne serait-ce qu'en raison de la répétition incessante d'un nombre d'images restreint - ne convient généralement pas aux façades médiatiques. L'évolution des conditions de la situation dans laquelle la mise en scène est perçue exige de nouveaux types de diffusion. Au-delà des diffusions classiques d'images ou de films, les médias numériques offrent des possibilités révolutionnaires utilisant des images qui s'auto-génèrent, des moyens interactifs et des réseaux qui répondent aux nouvelles exigences des mises en scène médiatiques sur les façades. Les projets décrits dans le présent ouvrage sont répartis en trois chapitres correspondant respectivement à trois types de diffusion différents : la mise en scène interactive, la mise en scène auto-active et la mise en scène réactive.

Tipos de escenificación

Como consecuencia del actual torrente de estímulos, la atención se ha convertido en un bien escaso. Las imágenes en movimiento en una fachada ofrecen, en este sentido, una ventaja decisiva: desde el punto de vista de la psicología de la percepción, cada movimiento –desencadenado por un reflejo natural de orientación– dirige nuestra atención hacia él. En cambio, las imágenes estáticas desaparecen con el tiempo del enfoque de la percepción humana.

La adecuada escenificación de una fachada mediática ha de resultar acorde con la forma del edificio. La arquitectura y los contenidos de la escenificación se influyen recíprocamente y se perciben como un todo: el edificio se muestra como un organismo vivo. Si además los contenidos y los eventos del propio edificio se representan en la fachada, se produce una comunicación entre éste y lo mostrado. Esa correlación genera una unidad: el interior se vuelca hacia fuera en la fachada.

Medios visuales clásicos como el cine o la televisión disponen, por un lado, de un amplio fondo de material visual, en crecimiento constante, con un costoso aparato redaccional y, por otro, de la posibilidad de que el espectador seleccione un programa. El caso de las fachadas mediáticas es distinto. Dada su presencia estática en el espacio urbano, son un componente integral de la cotidianidad urbana de un gran número de personas, que conviven con la fachada mediática las veinticuatro horas del día, todos los días del año. En la mayoría de los casos, una escenificación con los anuncios publicitarios clásicos no satisface las pretensiones de estas fachadas –aunque sólo sea por la mera repetición constante de un fondo limitado de material visual–. Las condiciones que crea esta alteración de la situación perceptiva exigen formas de puesta en escena más novedosas. Más allá de los recursos visuales y cinematográficos clásicos, los medios digitales ofrecen aquí otras posibilidades que son más acordes a los nuevos requerimientos de las fachadas mediáticas, ya que permiten la generación propia de imágenes, la interacción y la integración en la red. Atendiendo a los tres tipos de escenificación: interactiva, autoactiva y reactiva, los proyectos de este libro se presentan en tres capítulos.

Tipologie di messa in scena

A causa del bombardamento di stimoli a cui tutti siamo sottoposti, l'attenzione è una risorsa sempre più rara. In questo senso, le immagini in movimento su una facciata dinamica presentano un vantaggio fondamentale: dal punto di vista della psicologia della percezione, ogni movimento provocato da un riflesso naturale di orientamento finisce per attirare l'attenzione. Viceversa, le immagini statiche scompaiono col tempo dal centro della percezione umana.

L'adeguata messa in scena di una facciata mediatica si armonizza pienamente con l'aspetto formale dell'edificio. Architettura e contenuti presentati si influenzano a vicenda e vengono percepiti come un insieme unico: l'edificio si mostra come organismo vivo. Se ora i contenuti e gli eventi all'interno dell'edificio vengono messi in scena sulla facciata, edifici e messa in scena entrano in comunicazione. Un effetto reciproco che genera un'unità – l'interno si rivolge all'esterno attraverso la facciata.

I mezzi di comunicazione visiva classici, come il cinema o la televisione, dispongono sia di una vasta scelta, (in costante crescita), di materiale iconografico, con un costoso apparato redazionale alle spalle, sia della possibilità di scelta del programma da parte di chi guarda. Per le facciate mediatiche è completamente diverso. Esse diventano, a causa della loro presenza stazionaria nello spazio cittadino, un elemento integrante della quotidianità urbana per un gran numero di persone, le quali vivono la facciata mediatica 24 ore al giorno, per tutto l'anno. Nella maggioranza dei casi, la messa in scena di una facciata con il classico filmato pubblicitario non è più adeguata alle esigenze della facciata mediatica, fosse anche solo a causa della costante ripetizione di una quantità limitata di materiale iconografico. Le condizioni di base di questa situazione modificata di percezione esigono nuove modalità di messa in scena. Oltre alle messe in scena classiche, con l'impiego di immagini e filmati, i mezzi di comunicazione digitali offrono in questo caso nuove possibilità grazie a immagini autogenerate, strumenti interattivi e collegamenti in rete, che rispondono meglio alle necessità in divenire della messa in scena delle facciate mediatiche. I progetti raccolti in questo libro sono suddivisi in tre capitoli in base alle tre modalità di messa in scena, interattiva, autoattiva e reattiva.

INTERACTIVE PROGRAMMING

INTERAKTIVE BESPIELUNG

LA MISE EN SCÈNE INTERACTIVE

ESCENIFICACIÓN INTERACTIVA

MESSA IN SCENA INTERATTIVA

High degree of identification through playful interaction

The options to interact and participate belongs to the pivotal attributes of digital media. The involvement of users and visitors into the media programme of the building increases both perception of and identification with the media facade and its contents. The possibility of playful interaction or creative participation makes the media facade to an integral item of the urban environment that displays a whole variety of uses.

Interactive displays are not only exciting for the active participant but also for the passive audience. Even classic video games such as Pong or Pac-Man, both stemming from the early 80s, fascinate to this day despite their relatively simple interaction. New interfaces such as the mobile phone, laptop, PDA and other mobile electronic equipment extend the spectrum of interactive possibilities. In combination with a media facade, camera recognition or an interface directly in front of the facade create a totally new and exciting spatial dimension.

Hohe Identifikation durch spielerische Interaktion

Die Option zur Interaktion und Partizipation gehört zu den entscheidenden Merkmalen der digitalen Medien. Werden Nutzer und Besucher in die mediale Bespielung des Gebäudes mit einbezogen, steigert dies die Wahrnehmung und Identifikation mit der Medienfassade und ihren Inhalten. Durch die Möglichkeit zur spielerischen Interaktion oder gestalterischen Partizipation wird die Medienfassade integraler und vielfältig genutzter Bestandteil des städtischen Umfeldes.

Dabei ist eine interaktive Bespielung sowohl für den aktiven Teilnehmer als auch für den passiven Beobachter spannend. Selbst klassische Videospiele wie Pong oder Pacman, die bereits Anfang der 80er Jahre entwickelt wurden, lösen trotz ihrer einfachen Interaktion noch heute eine große Faszination aus. Neue Schnittstellen wie z.B. Handy, Laptop, PDA und andere mobile Datengeräte erweitern das Spektrum der Interaktionsmöglichkeiten. In Kombination mit einer Medienfassade schaffen eine Kameraerkennung oder ein Interface direkt vor der Fassade eine völlig neue und spannende räumliche Dimension.

Forte identification grâce au principe d'interaction ludique

L'option de l'interaction et de la participation est l'une des principales caractéristiques des médias numériques. Quand les occupants et les visiteurs sont associés à la mise en scène médiatique du bâtiment, ils perçoivent et s'identifient plus fortement à la façade médiatique et à ce qu'elle diffuse. L'interaction ludique ou la participation créatrice font de la façade médiatique un élément exploité de manière intégrale et variée dans le paysage urbain.

La mise en scène interactive est tout aussi passionnante pour le participant actif que pour le spectateur passif. Même les jeux vidéo classiques tels que Pong ou Pacman, qui ont été développés au début des années 80, fascinent aujourd'hui encore le public malgré la simplicité de leur interaction. De nouvelles interfaces, notamment les téléphones ou les ordinateurs portables, les PDA et autres technologies mobiles, multiplient les possibilités d'interaction. La présence d'une caméra ou d'une interface juste devant la façade médiatique crée – en association avec cette dernière – une dimension spatiale entièrement nouvelle et tout à fait passionnante.

Alto grado de identificación a través de una interacción lúdica

Uno de los rasgos más destacados de los medios digitales es que optan por la interacción y la participación. Si se implica a los usuarios y visitantes en la puesta en escena del edificio, aumenta la percepción de la fachada mediática y la identificación con sus contenidos. Con la posibilidad de la interacción lúdica o participación creativa, la fachada mediática se convierte en un componente integral de aplicaciones múltiples del entorno urbano.

Hay que considerar, además, que una escenificación interactiva es interesante tanto para los participantes activos como para los observadores pasivos. Videojuegos clásicos como Pong o Pacman, que se concibieron en los inicios de la década de 1980, siguen produciendo aun hoy una gran fascinación pese a su sencilla interacción. Nuevas interfaces como por ejemplo móviles, portátiles, agendas electrónicas y otras unidades terminales móviles amplían el espectro de las posibilidades de la interacción. En combinación con una fachada mediática, un visualizador de imágenes o una interfaz consiguen una dimensión espacial completamente nueva y sugestiva.

Profondità d'identificazione attraverso l'interazione ludica

La scelta dell'interazione e della partecipazione fa parte delle caratteristiche fondamentali dei media digitali. Se utente e visitatore vengono compresi nella messa in scena mediatica dell'edificio, aumentano la percezione e l'identificazione con la facciata mediatica e con il suo contenuto. Attraverso la possibilità dell'interazione giocosa o della partecipazione creativa, la facciata mediatica diventa parte integrante e utilizzata in più modi dell'ambiente urbano.

In questo senso, la messa in scena interattiva è un'emozione sia per chi partecipa attivamente che per l'osservatore passivo. Anche i videogiochi classici, come Pong o Pacman, già collaudati all'inizio degli anni Ottanta, nonostante la semplicità dell'interazione esercitano ancora oggi una grande attrattiva. Nuove interfacce, come il telefono cellulare, il computer portatile e il palmare, nonché altri supporti dati mobili, ampliano ulteriormente la gamma delle possibilità di interazione. In abbinamento a una facciata mediatica, una videocamera a sensori di movimento o un'interfaccia poste direttamente davanti alla facciata creano una dimensione spaziale totalmente nuova ed emozionante.

CAMPUS
T-MOBILE HEADQUARTERS | BONN
Realisation: 2004
Architect: Professor Peter Schmitz, Cologne

T-Mobile expanded its headquarters in Bonn in 2003 to include a company campus providing some 5,000 jobs. The result is a central building with a dual function: as forum for events and as main entrance with reception lobby. T-Mobile was looking for a special kind of staging for its campus. It ideally should present the company logo on the front of the main building in an innovative way.

ag4 built the world's first transparent media facade for T-Mobile. It is a horizontal panel construction covering some 300 square metres which is attached to the actual glass facade. The panels have integrated LEDs, ensuring the building displays full media capabilities. The distances between the single panels provide a clear view of the campus from the inside. The view from the square reveals the inner space superimposed by the electronic image. The transparency which can be perceived from both the inside and the outside is responsible for the special kind of magic of the transparent media facade. The potential of the transparent media facade has surpassed T-Mobile's greatest expectations: not only does the facade animate the company's logo, but the entire brand is staged by means of moving images and videos.

The square in front of the media facade of the T-Mobile Campus turns into an interactive playground. A camera records the movements on the square which are directly incorporated into the display of the media facade. This makes it feasible to have a joint video game during lunch break: two players standing on the square can control their digital racquets on the media facade with which they play a ball back and forth. It is even possible to display personal images via mobile phone or the Internet – in an edited version – on the facade.

The basic display on the facade is a real-time self-generating programme which plays with the architecture of the T-Mobile building and the company's CI. The basic display is complemented by single, event-related sequences which can be animated, auto-active films that draw the viewer's attention to current events on the T-Mobile Campus. Another example is the Tour de France: the cyclists of the T-Mobile team are animated large scale and incorporated into the current display while a live ticker informs the viewer of the latest news and events from the current stage and is updated every minute. Further programmes related to the Tour de France show the previous day's highlights and the single stage profiles.

2003 erweiterte T-Mobile sein Headquarter in Bonn zu einem Firmencampus, der Arbeitsplätze für 5.000 Mitarbeiter bietet. In diesem Rahmen entstand ein zentraler Bau mit einer Doppelfunktion: als Forum für Veranstaltungen und als Haupteingang mit Empfangsfunktion. T-Mobile suchte für seinen Campus eine besondere Inszenierung. Gewünscht war ein innovativer Weg, das Firmenlogo auf der Fassade des Hauptgebäudes zu präsentieren.

ag4 baute für T-Mobile die erste Transparente Medienfassade der Welt. Als horizontale Lamellenkonstruktion ist sie mit einer Fläche von 300 m^2 vor die bestehende Glasfassade montiert. In die Lamellen sind Leuchtdioden integriert, die eine mediale Bespielung der Architektur ermöglichen. Der Abstand zwischen den Lamellen gewährleistet einen freien Blick vom Inneren des Gebäudes auf den Campusplatz. Vom Platz aus betrachtet überlagert sich das elektronische Bild mit dem Blick in die Räume der Architektur. Die sowohl von Innen als auch von Außen wahrgenommene Transparenz macht die besondere Magie der Transparenten Medienfassade aus. Das Potenzial der Transparenten Medienfassade übertraf die Erwartungen bei T-Mobile: Es wird nicht nur das Firmenlogo animiert, sondern die gesamte Marke in bewegten Bildern und Videos innovativ inszeniert.

Der Platz vor der Medienfassade des T-Mobile-Campus wird zur interaktiven Spielwiese. Eine Kameraerkennung erfasst die Bewegungen auf dem Platz, die dann als Parameter direkt in die Bespielung der Medienfassade einfließen können. So ist es möglich, die Mittagspause mit einem gemeinschaftlichen Pong-Spiel zu verbringen: zwei Spieler steuern nur durch ihre Bewegung auf dem Platz zwei digitale Balken auf der Medienfassade, mit denen sie sich einen digitalen Ball zuspielen. Über das Handy oder das Internet können persönliche Bilder – redaktionell betreut – auf die Fassade gespielt werden.

Die Basisbespielung der Fassade ist ein sich in Echtzeit selbst generierendes Programm, das sowohl mit der Architektur als auch der CI von T-Mobile spielt. Aufbauend auf der Basisbespielung werden einzelne, eventbezogene Bespielungen integriert. Dies können animierte, autoaktive Filme sein, die auf aktuelle Veranstaltungen auf dem T-Mobile Campus hinweisen. Ein anderes Beispiel ist die Dokumentation der Tour de France: Die Fahrer des T-Mobile-Teams werden großflächig animiert in das Bespielungsprogramm eingebunden und ein Live-Ticker informiert im Minutentakt über die neuesten Ereignisse der laufenden Etappe. Weitere Bespielungen zur Tour de France zeigen die Höhepunkte des Vortages sowie die einzelnen Etappenprofile.

En 2003, l'entreprise T-Mobile a agrandi son siège à Bonn et l'a transformé en véritable campus industriel pour 5 000 employés. La construction née de ce cadre possède une double fonction : elle représente d'une part un forum de manifestations et d'autre part l'entrée principale du campus avec hall d'accueil. T-Moblie souhaitait mettre son campus en scène avec originalité. L'entreprise était à la recherche d'un moyen novateur pour présenter son logo de l'entreprise sur la façade du bâtiment principal.

ag4 a réalisé pour T-Mobile la première façade médiatique transparente au monde. La construction de 300 mètres carrés est composée de lamelles horizontales placées devant la façade en verre du bâtiment. Des DEL intégrées aux lamelles permettent de faire défiler des diffusions médiatiques sur l'architecture. Grâce aux intervalles entre les lamelles, la vue sur la place du campus reste intacte depuis l'intérieur du bâtiment. De la place, l'image électronique se fond avec la vue vers l'intérieur du bâtiment. Cette impression de transparence, perçue aussi bien depuis l'intérieur que depuis l'extérieur du bâtiment, est ce qui rend les façades médiatiques transparentes si fascinantes. Le potentiel de la façade transparente médiatique a surpassé les attentes de T-Mobile : l'animation du logo s'est transformée en véritable mise en scène de toute la marque sur la base d'images animées et de vidéos.

La place située devant la façade médiatique du campus T-Mobile est transformée en aire de jeux médiatique. Une caméra enregistre les mouvements qui ont lieu sur la place et les transmet directement sous forme de paramètres à la façade médiatique pour les intégrer à la diffusion. Ainsi, on peut passer sa pause du déjeuner à disputer une partie de Pong avec un collègue : grâce aux mouvements qu'ils effectuent sur la place, les deux joueurs commandent deux barres numériques représentées sur la façade médiatique et avec lesquelles ils se renvoient une balle numérique. A l'aide d'un téléphone portable ou d'un accès Internet, on peut même faire diffuser des images personnelles sur la façade médiatique – sous contrôle rédactionnel.

La mise en scène de base de la façade est un programme auto-généré en temps réel, qui joue aussi bien avec l'architecture qu'avec l'identité d'entreprise de T-Mobile. Des mises en scène individuelles et associées à des évènements particuliers sont intégrées à la diffusion de base. Il peut s'agir de films animés ou auto-actifs attirant l'attention sur les manifestations actuelles se déroulant sur le campus de T-Mobile. Un autre exemple est la documentation du Tour de France: les coureurs de l'équipe T-Mobile sont intégrés en grand format au programme faisant l'objet de la diffusion et un message défilant informe toutes les minutes des dernières actualités de l'étape en direct du tour. D'autres diffusions du Tour de France montrent les moments forts de la veille et les différents profils d'étapes.

En 2003, T-Mobile amplió su sede central en Bonn para convertirla en un campus de empresas que ofrece puestos de trabajo a 5.000 empleados. En ese marco surgió una edificación centralizada con un doble cometido: foro de los distintos actos organizados y entrada principal con funciones de recepción. T-Mobile buscaba una puesta en escena original del campus y un modo innovador de presentar su logotipo en la fachada del edificio principal.

ag4 construyó para T-Mobile la primera fachada mediática transparente del mundo. Ésta, una construcción de láminas horizontales con una superficie de 300 metros cuadrados, está montada delante de la fachada de vidrio existente. Las láminas llevan integrados diodos luminiscentes que permiten una escenificación mediática de la arquitectura. La distancia entre las láminas asegura una visión libre de la plaza del campus desde el interior del edificio. Observada desde la plaza, la imagen electrónica se superpone a la visión de los espacios arquitectónicos. La transparencia, percibida tanto desde dentro como desde fuera, confiere a la fachada mediática su magia especial. El potencial de la fachada resultante supera las expectativas de T-Mobile: no sólo el logotipo tiene animación sino toda la marca en imágenes y vídeos dinámicos exhibidos de forma innovadora.

La plaza situada delante de la fachada mediática del campus de T-Mobile se convierte en una zona de juego interactiva. Un visualizador registra los movimientos que se producen en ella que, de ese modo, pueden introducirse como parámetros directamente en la escenificación de la fachada. Ello hace posible celebrar una partida de Pong comunitaria durante el descanso de mediodía: dos jugadores dirigen sólo con sus movimientos en la plaza dos recuadros digitales de la fachada mediática con los que se pasan una pelota digital. Por medio del móvil o internet, pueden llevarse imágenes personales –previamente editadas– a la fachada.

La escenificación de base de la fachada es un programa que se genera así mismo en tiempo real y que juega tanto con la arquitectura como con la identidad corporativa de T-Mobile. Como refuerzo de este programa se integran otros contenidos concretos referidos a lo que acontece, que pueden ser filmes autoactivos que aluden a los actos previstos en el campus de T-Mobile. Otra posibilidad es el seguimiento del Tour de Francia: los ciclistas del equipo de T-Mobile se muestran en movimiento a toda pantalla en la fachada, y un marcador en directo informa minuto a minuto sobre los avatares más recientes de la etapa actual. Otras trasmisiones sobre el Tour abordan los momentos culminantes del día anterior y los perfiles de las distintas etapas.

Nel 2003 T-Mobile ha ampliato la sede principale di Bonn con un campus aziendale, che ospita postazioni di lavoro per 5000 persone. In tale contesto è stato ricavato un edificio centrale con una duplice funzione: centro di manifestazioni ed eventi e ingresso principale con funzione di accoglienza. T-Mobile cercava per il Campus un colpo d'occhio particolare e un percorso innovativo, per presentare il logo aziendale sulla facciata dell'edificio principale.

ag4 ha creato per T-Mobile la prima facciata mediatica trasparente al mondo. Si presenta come una struttura a lamelle orizzontali, con una superficie di 300 metri quadrati, montata sulla facciata in vetro già esistente. Nelle lamelle sono integrati i LED luminosi, che consentono la messa in scena mediatica dell'architettura. La distanza tra le lamelle garantisce la possibilità di spaziare con lo sguardo dall'interno dell'edificio sull'area del Campus. Osservando dal piazzale antistante, l'immagine elettronica risulta sovrapposta agli spazi architettonici. La trasparenza percepita sia dall'interno che dall'esterno crea la particolare magia della facciata mediatica. Il potenziale della facciata mediatica trasparente ha superato le aspettative del committente: non è soltanto il logo aziendale a essere animato, ma è il marchio nel suo insieme che viene messo in scena in modo innovativo, attraverso immagini in movimento e filmati.

Lo spazio davanti alla facciata mediatica del Campus T-Mobile diventa un terreno di gioco interattivo. Una videocamera riprende i movimenti sul piazzale, che possono scorrere come parametro esterno direttamente nella messa in scena della facciata. Diventa così possibile trasformare la pausa pranzo in una partita di Pong aperta: due giocatori, semplicemente muovendosi sul piazzale, comandano due barre digitali sulla facciata mediatica, con le quali si palleggiano una pallina virtuale. Con il cellulare o attraverso Internet è possibile inviare alla facciata anche immagini personali, in questo caso con l'assistenza di una redazione.

La messa in scena di base della facciata è un programma autogenerato in tempo reale, che gioca sia con l'architettura che con il CI di T-Mobile. Sulla base di questa messa in scena vengono integrate singole messe in scena riferite a eventi particolari e sempre diversi. Possono essere filmati animati autoattivi, riferiti a manifestazioni che avvengono in quel momento nel Campus. Altro esempio è la documentazione del Tour de France: i corridori del team T-Mobile vengono animati a schermo intero, inseriti nel programma della messa in scena, mentre un messaggio variabile live fornisce informazioni minuto per minuto sugli ultimi avvenimenti della tappa in corso. Altri esempi relativi al Tour de France sono quelli che mostrano i punti salienti delle giornate precedenti e le caratteristiche delle singole tappe.

SCULPTURE
KHALIFA TOWER | DOHA
Concept: 2004/2005
Realisation: 2006

Doha will host the Asian Games in 2006, an occasion that calls for the building of a number of large stadiums. The Khalifa Tower, some 300 metres tall, will provide a spectacular and clearly visible sign of this architectural ensemble. The medialized tower emanates the positive spirit of the Asian Games into the whole world.

The tower has an open construction whose concrete core is coated with a stainless steel mesh. This mesh acts as a casing and dominates the tower's outer appearance. Differently sized, multi-storey ring modules provide the main structure of the tower.

Illumesh®

The entire tower's stainless steel mesh turns into a projection screen. This becomes possible because very slim construction rings of only a few centimetres thickness surround the tower at a horizontal interval of three metres. There is a fine grid of LEDs worked into these horizontal rings which serve to illuminate the entire mesh. The considerable variance in the vertical and horizontal LEDs creates an individual and attractive aesthetics – an effect accentuated by the reflections on the structured surface of the stainless steel mesh which creates an additional three-dimensional magic.

The tower's basic display measures some 22,000 square metres and consists of a play of colours and animated art designs which are atmospherically attuned to the colours of the current event. A possibility, for example, is the dynamic ascension of the Olympic rings. However, the tower can actually interact with the events: whenever the first athlete crosses the finishing line or a goal is scored the tower responds with medialised fireworks.

Mediamesh®

A transparent oval media facade with a size of 1,800 square metres is planned in the lower part of the tower. In this case the LEDs will be woven into the stainless steel to enable an artistic and constructive integration of the medialized area into the overall appearance of the tower. The high resolution is capable of video content which can be read from a distance as little as 100 metres.

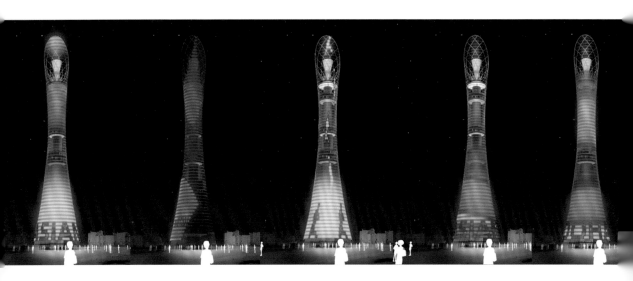

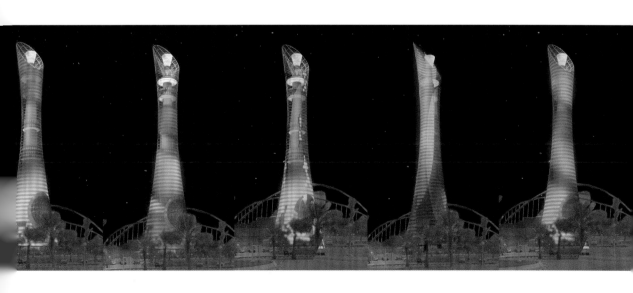

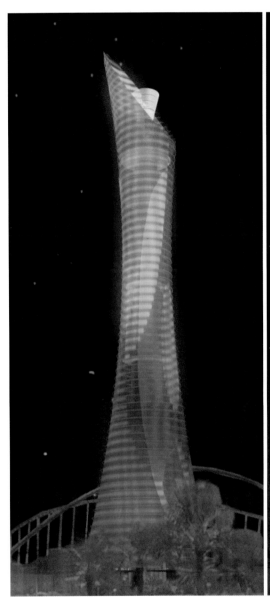

2006 finden in Doha die Asian Games statt. Zu diesem Anlass wird eine Reihe großer Stadien gebaut. Ein 300 Meter hoher Tower, der Khalifa Tower, wird in diesem architektonischen Ensemble ein weithin sichtbares, spektakuläres Zeichen bilden. Medialisiert strahlt er den positiven Geist der Asian Games in die ganze Welt.

Der Tower besteht aus einer offenen Konstruktion, dessen Betonkern mit einem Edelstahlgewebe überzogen ist. Das Edelstahlgewebe bildet als vorgespannte Hülle die äußere Form des Towers. Unterschiedlich dimensionierte, mehr-geschossige Ringmodule gliedern den Tower.

Illumesh®

Das Edelstahlgewebe des gesamten Towers wird zur Projektionsfläche der Bespielung. Dies wird möglich, indem sich in einem vertikalen Abstand von drei Metern wenige Zentimeter schlanke Konstruktionsringe um den Tower schichten. In diese horizontalen Ringe sind in einem engen Raster LEDs integriert, mit denen das Gewebe vollflächig illuminiert wird. Der stark unterschiedliche Abstand in der Vertikalen und der Horizontalen der LED-Bildpunkte erzeugt dabei eine eigene, reizvolle Ästhetik, wobei die Lichtreflektionen auf der Struktur der Oberfläche des Edelstahlgewebes eine zusätzliche, dreidimensionale Magie schaffen.

Die Basisbespielung des Towers, 22.000qm groß, besteht aus Farbspielen und animierten Grafiken, die mit den Farben der jeweiligen Veranstaltung atmosphärisch spielen. Möglich ist hier beispielsweise das dynamische Aufsteigen der Olympischen Ringe. Der Tower kann mit den Veranstaltungen jedoch auch in Interaktion treten: läuft ein Sportler als Sieger über die Zielgerade oder schießt ein Tor, reagiert der Tower mit einem medialisierten Feuerwerk.

Mediamesh®

Im unteren Bereich des Towers ist eine ovale Transparente Medienfassade in einer Größe von 1800qm geplant. Hierfür werden LEDs in das Edelstahlgewebe eingewebt. So ist eine gestalterische und konstruktive Integration der medialisierten Fläche in die Gesamterscheinung des Towers möglich. Die hohe Auflösung ermöglicht eine Videobespielung, die schon in einer Entfernung von 100m lesbar ist.

En 2006, les Jeux Asiatiques se dérouleront à Doha. Cette manifestation est à l'origine de la construction de toute une série de grands stades. Une tour haute de 300 mètres, la «Khalifa Tower», représentera dans cet ensemble architectonique un symbole spectaculaire qui sera visible de très loin. La mise en scène médiatique dont elle fera l'objet lui permettra de véhiculer l'esprit positif des Jeux Asiatiques dans le monde entier.

La tour est une construction ouverte composée d'un noyau en béton recouvert d'une toile métallique en acier fin noble. Cette toile métallique recouvre la forme extérieure de la tour comme une enveloppe tendue. La tour se divise en modules de différentes tailles composés d'anneaux à plusieurs étages.

Illumesh®

Toute la toile métallique de la tour devient le support de base de la mise en scène médiatique. Cela est rendu possible grâce à la présence, tout autour de la tour, d'anneaux de construction horizontaux de quelques centimètres d'épaisseur, espacés les uns des autres de 3 mètres. Des LED à trame serrée sont installés dans ces anneaux horizontaux, permettant d'illuminer la toile métallique sur toute sa surface. L'écart très différent entre les points d'image LED verticaux et horizontaux crée une esthétique attrayante, et les reflets lumineux sur la structure de la surface de la toile métallique produisent un effet supplémentaire de magie tridimensionnelle.

La mise en scène de base de la tour, sur une surface de 22 000 mètres carrés, est composée de jeux de couleurs et d'images animées en relation avec les couleurs et l'atmosphère de chaque manifestation. Il est possible, par exemple, de représenter une ascension dynamique des anneaux olympiques. La tour peut également interagir avec les différentes manifestations : lorsqu'un sportif traverse en vainqueur la ligne d'arrivée ou marque un but, la tour réagit avec un feu d'artifice médiatique.

Mediamesh®

Dans la partie inférieure de la tour, il est prévu d'installer une façade médiatique transparente ovale de 1 800 mètres carrés. A cet effet, des DEL ont été tissées dans la toile métallique, permettant d'intégrer de façon créative et constructive la surface de la mise en scène médiatique à l'aspect global de la tour. La haute résolution permet de diffuser des vidéos perceptibles à partir d'une distance de 100 mètres.

En 2006 se celebrarán en Doha los Juegos Asiáticos. Para la ocasión se está construyendo una serie de grandes estadios. La Khalifa Tower, un rascacielos de 300 metros de altura, constituirá en ese marco arquitectónico un espectacular punto de referencia visible a gran distancia. Con la ayuda mediática emite el espíritu positivo de los Juegos Asiáticos a todo el mudo.

El rascacielos es una construcción abierta con un núcleo de hormigón recubierto por un tejido de acero. El tejido de acero, como envoltura pretensionada, confiere al edificio su forma exterior, y módulos circulares de distintas dimensiones y varios pisos lo estructuran.

Illumesh®

El tejido de acero del rascacielos hace de superficie de proyección de la puesta en escena. Ello se consigue disponiendo alrededor del edificio anillos de construcción de pocos centímetros de grosor con una separación vertical de tres metros. En estos anillos horizontales están integrados en una estrecha retícula LEDs con los que se ilumina toda la superficie del tejido. La gran diferencia de distancia entre los píxeles LED verticales y los horizontales compone una estética particularmente atractiva, en la que los reflejos de luz en la estructura superficial del tejido de acero generan una magia tridimensional añadida.

La escenificación de base del rascacielos, de 20.000 metros cuadrados, consta de repertorios lumínicos e imágenes móviles que juegan atmosféricamente con los colores de los actos correspondientes. Así, por ejemplo, es posible mostrar un ascenso dinámico de los anillos olímpicos. Pero, además, el rascacielos interacciona con los distintos eventos: en el momento en que un deportista llega a la línea de meta o mete un gol, el rascacielos reacciona con un castillo de fuegos artificiales mediático.

Mediamesh®

En la parte inferior del rascacielos está previsto instalar una fachada mediática transparente oval de 1.800 metros cuadrados de extensión. Para ello se intercalarán LEDs en el tejido de acero. Así se logra una integración creativa y constructiva de la superficie mediatizada en la imagen de conjunto del rascacielos. La alta resolución permite emisiones de vídeo, legibles a una distancia de 100 metros.

Nel 2006 si svolgeranno a Doha, nel Qatar, i Giochi Asiatici. Per l'occasione è in via di costruzione una serie di grandi stadi. Una torre alta 300 metri, la Khalifa Tower, costituirà in questo contesto architettonico un punto d'attrazione spettacolare, visibile da lontano. Una volta medializzata, sarà in grado di trasmettere lo spirito positivo dei Giochi Asiatici in tutto il mondo.

La Tower è una costruzione aperta, con un nucleo in cemento rivestito da un reticolato di acciaio inox. È questo reticolato, applicato come una copertura, a costituire la forma esterna della torre. Moduli circolari a più piani, di dimensioni diverse, articolano la torre.

Illumesh®

Il reticolato in acciaio dell'intera torre diventa lo schermo di proiezione della messa in scena. Ciò diviene possibile in quanto, distanziati di tre metri l'uno dall'altro, sono stati disposti anelli larghi pochi centimetri tutto attorno alla torre. In questi anelli orizzontali sono integrati i LED in un fitta maglia metallica, in modo che la struttura in acciaio ne risulti completamente coperta e illuminata. La differenza di distanza tra i componenti verticali e orizzontali della rete di LED produce un'estetica particolare e di grande impatto, mentre i riflessi di luce sulla struttura superficiale del reticolato d'acciaio creano un'ulteriore magia tridimensionale.

La messa in scena di base della torre, con una superficie di 22.000 metri quadrati, è costituita da giochi di colori e grafiche animate, che interagiscono con i colori delle condizioni atmosferiche momento per momento. In questo caso è possibile, ad esempio, la rappresentazione dinamica degli anelli olimpici. La torre può altresì interagire con gli eventi del momento: quando un atleta taglia per primo il traguardo o un calciatore tira un goal in porta, la torre reagisce con un fuoco d'artificio virtuale.

Mediamesh®

Nella fascia inferiore della torre è installata una facciata mediatica trasparente di 1800 metri quadrati. A questo scopo, i LED sono stati letteralmente "intessuti" nel reticolato d'acciaio. In questo modo è possibile realizzare un'integrazione, creativa e costruttiva allo stesso tempo, della superficie medializzata nell'aspetto complessivo della torre. L'immagine ad alta risoluzione consente la messa in scena di videofilmati, visibili a una distanza di 100 metri.

FATA MORGANA
MAIN RAILWAY STATION | COLOGNE
Concept: 2004

During the course of an ideas competition by the Bauhaus Dessau on the subject of "Transit", ag4 developed a concept for the medialisation of Cologne's main railway station.

The architecture of Cologne's main railway station with its large scale glass facade enables a clear view from the inside of the building onto the city's landmark – Cologne Cathedral. As an area dedicated to transit, the main railway station is the hub for arrivals, departures and through-journeys. The central idea of the concept envisages to greet the traveller with the place of his or her departure as he or she arrives.

This is made possible by a transparent media facade which is installed in front of the entire glass façade and faces the station's main arrival and departure hall. The media facade consists of panels with in-built LEDs with a vertical clearance of 10 centimetres. The traveller will experience a completely media image from as little a distance as 10 metres. As he or she approaches the media image will begin to make way to the space behind the facade – the forecourt of Cologne Cathedral.

The images on display interact with the arrival of main-line trains. When a main-line train arrives, the announcement on the media facade communicates the train's arrival and its station of departure. This is followed by a live film of that station's foyer, for example, the forecourt of Frankfurt's main railway station.

The arriving passenger enters the main foyer in Cologne and suddenly feels as though he/she is back from where he/she came. The place of origin travelled with him/her as a memory and appears to him/her as an after-image, as a mirage. As the traveller approaches the exit this mirage becomes fainter and fainter while the point of arrival – Cologne – starts to dominate and becomes real.

For those people waiting in the main foyer the media facade creates the vision of the main station as a hub for international transit.

Im Rahmen eines vom Bauhaus Dessau ausgeschriebenen Ideenwettbewerbs zum Thema „Transit" entwickelte ag4 ein Konzept für die Medialisierung des Kölner Hauptbahnhofs.

Die Architektur des Kölner Hauptbahnhofs ermöglicht mit ihrer großen Glasfassade in der Haupthalle den freien Blick auf das Wahrzeichen von Köln – den Kölner Dom. Als Transitraum ist der Hauptbahnhof die Drehscheibe für Ankunft, Abreise und Durchreise. Die zentrale Idee des Konzepts sieht vor, den ankommenden Reisenden noch einmal mit dem Ort seiner Abreise zu begrüßen, wenn er seinen neuen Ankunftsort betritt.

Möglich ist dies durch eine Transparente Medienfassade, die von Innen und dem Raum im Bahnhof zugewandt vor die gesamte Glasfassade installiert ist. Die Medienfassade besteht aus LED-Bildpunkten in Lamellen mit einem vertikalen Abstand von 10 Zentimetern. Ein vollständig medialisiertes Bild erscheint dem Reisenden ab einem Betrachtungsabstand von 10 Metern. Je näher der Reisende der Fassade kommt, desto mehr löst sich das medialisierte Bild auf und der Blick auf den Raum hinter der Fassade, den Vorplatz mit dem Kölner Dom, legt sich frei.

Die Bespielung der Medienfassade interagiert mit den ankommenden Fernzügen. Fährt ein Fernzug ein, kommuniziert ein Schriftzug auf der Medienfassade die Ankunft des Zuges und seinen Abfahrtsbahnhof. Danach erscheint ein Live-Film aus der Empfangshalle desjenigen Bahnhofs, von dem der betreffende Zug abgefahren ist – z.B. der Vorplatz des Frankfurter Hauptbahnhofs.

Der ankommende Reisende betritt die Empfangshalle in Köln und hat das Gefühl, plötzlich wieder an seinem Abfahrtsort angekommen zu sein. Der Ort der Abfahrt ist als Erinnerung mit ihm gereist und erscheint als Nachbild wie eine Fata Morgana. Je näher der Reisende dem Ausgang kommt, desto mehr verschwindet dieses Nachbild – der neue Ankunftsort Köln wird real.

Für die Menschen, die in der Haupthalle warten, schafft die Medienfassade ein Bild des Bahnhofs als international vernetzter Transitort.

Dans le cadre d'un concours d'idées organisé par le Bauhaus de Dessau sur le thème « Transit », ag4 a mis au point un concept de mise en scène médiatique de la Gare centrale de Cologne.

Grâce à sa grande façade en verre située dans le hall principal, l'architecture de la Gare centrale de Cologne offre une vue dégagée sur la cathédrale de Cologne - l'emblème de la ville. La Gare centrale, espace de transit, représente la plaque tournante des arrivées, départs et passages des voyageurs. L'idée centrale du concept consiste à confronter une nouvelle fois le voyageur qui arrive en gare avec son lieu de départ, et ce au moment exact où il arrive à destination.

Ce processus est rendu possible grâce à une façade médiatique transparente installée devant la façade en verre, à l'intérieur de la gare, et tournée vers le hall d'entrée. La façade médiatique est composée de points d'images sous forme de DEL placées dans des lamelles verticales espacées de 10 cm les unes des autres. Une image entièrement médialisée apparaît au voyageur à partir d'une distance d'observation de 10 mètres. Plus le voyageur se rapproche de la façade, plus l'image médialisée se dissipe pour laisser apparaître l'espace situé derrière la façade, c'est-à-dire l'esplanade de la gare et la cathédrale de Cologne.

Le système de mise en scène de la façade médiatique interagit avec les trains des grandes lignes arrivant en gare. Lorsqu'un train entre en gare, un message s'affiche sur la façade médiatique pour annoncer l'arrivée du train et sa gare de départ. Ensuite, un film apparaît en provenance directe du hall d'accueil de la gare de laquelle est parti le train en question – par exemple depuis l'esplanade de la Gare centrale de Francfort.

Le voyageur qui arrive à Cologne a tout à coup l'impression d'être retourné sur son lieu de départ. La ville qu'il a quittée l'a accompagné sous forme de souvenir pendant toute la durée de son voyage et apparaît devant lui comme un mirage. Plus le voyageur se rapproche de la sortie, plus le mirage s'estompe – et sa véritable ville de destination, Cologne, devient véritablement réelle.

Pour les personnes qui attendent dans le hall principal, la façade médiatique transforme la gare en un lieu de transit relié à un réseau international.

En el marco de un concurso de ideas en torno al tema "tránsito" convocado por la Bauhaus de Dessau, ag4 desarrolló un concepto para la mediatización de la estación central de ferrocarril de Colonia.

La arquitectura de la estación central de Colonia, con una amplia fachada de vidrio, no opone ningún obstáculo a la visión del símbolo más emblemático de Colonia - su catedral, el Dom. Como zona de tránsito, la estación central es plataforma de llegadas, salidas y escalas. La idea medular del concepto prevé saludar a los viajeros recién llegados con el lugar en que han iniciado su viaje cuando entren en la estación de destino.

Esto es posible gracias a una fachada mediática transparente que, desde dentro y orientada al espacio de la estación, está instalada delante de toda la fachada de vidrio. La fachada mediática consta de píxeles LED integrados en láminas verticales separadas entre sí diez centímetros. Contemplada a partir de una distancia de diez metros, ante el viajero aparece una imagen plenamente mediática. A medida que éste se acerca a la fachada, la imagen se va difuminando cada vez más, quedando así libre a la vista el espacio que hay tras ella, la plaza con la catedral de Colonia.

La escenificación de la fachada mediática interactúa con los trenes de larga distancia que llegan: cuando uno hace su entrada, un rótulo comunica en la fachada su llegada y la estación de la que procede. Después aparece un filme en directo con imágenes de la estación de la que el tren ha partido –por ejemplo, la entrada de la estación central de ferrocarril de Fráncfort–.

El viajero recién llegado accede al vestíbulo de la estación de Colonia y tiene la impresión de haber vuelto repentinamente a su punto de origen. El lugar de partida ha viajado con él en el recuerdo y aparece, a modo de reproducción, como si de un espejismo se tratase. A medida que el viajero se acerca a la salida, la reproducción se dispersa progresivamente: Colonia, el lugar de destino, adquiere dimensión real.

Para las personas que esperan en la nave principal, la fachada mediática trasmite una imagen de la estación como lugar de tránsito conectado internacionalmente.

Nell'ambito di un concorso di idee bandito dalla fondazione Bauhaus Dessau sul tema "Transito", ag4 ha sviluppato un progetto per la medializzazione della Stazione Centrale di Colonia.

L'architettura della Stazione Centrale di Colonia, con la sua ampia facciata in vetro nella sala principale, consente di spaziare liberamente con lo sguardo sul simbolo della città, il Duomo. In quanto luogo di transito, la Stazione Centrale è uno snodo fondamentale per arrivi, partenze e passaggi. L'idea alla base del progetto prevede di accogliere il viaggiatore in arrivo ancora una volta con il luogo da cui è partito.

Ciò diventa possibile con una facciata mediatica trasparente installata all'interno del salone centrale della stazione, davanti alla facciata in vetro esistente. La facciata mediatica è costituita da LED posizionati in lamelle, distanziate in verticale di 10 centimetri. Al viaggiatore appare un'immagine completamente medializzata a una distanza di osservazione di 10 metri. Più ci si avvicina alla facciata, più si perde allo sguardo l'immagine medializzata, e l'occhio può spaziare liberamente oltre la facciata, fino alla piazza con il Duomo.

La messa in scena della facciata mediatica interagisce inoltre con i treni a lunga percorrenza in arrivo. Quando il treno è nei pressi della stazione, un messaggio sulla facciata mediatica ne comunica l'arrivo e la stazione di partenza. Quindi appare una ripresa live della sala principale della stazione di partenza del treno, ad esempio dell'atrio della Stazione Centrale di Francoforte.

Il viaggiatore in arrivo entra quindi nell'atrio della stazione di Colonia e ha la sensazione di essere tornato al luogo di partenza. Egli ha portato con sé nel ricordo il luogo da cui è partito, e questo gli appare sotto forma di immagine, come un miraggio. Ma più egli si avvicina all'uscita, più l'immagine si fa indistinta, fino a che si concretizza in tutta la sua realtà il nuovo luogo d'arrivo, Colonia.

Per coloro che attendono nell'atrio, la facciata mediatica crea un'immagine della stazione come luogo di transito, al centro di una rete internazionale.

LIFE
SERONO HEADQUARTERS | GENEVA
Concept: 2004/05
Realisation: 2006
Architect: Helmut Jahn

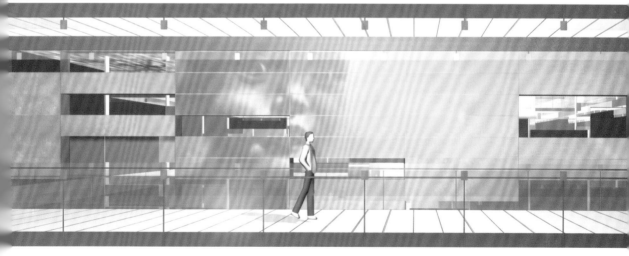

Serono is one of the world's leading pharmaceutical companies in the area of biotechnology and is in the process of expanding its headquarters in Geneva.

Helmut Jahn's architectural concept integrates the already existing old structure into the new company headquarters. A firewall of the old building turns into one side of an atrium which is to be part of the new and representative foyer.

Helmut Jahn asked ag4 mediatecture company® for a concept which would stage Serono's contextual focus media-tectonically in the area of the firewall.

Layers of Life

ag4 created a spatial installation consisting of a number of different layers. Modules made from pure bees' wax typify the layer as genetic code. LEDs are integrated into the wax modules which enable the medial function of the installation. The space between the firewall and the level with the wax modules is filled with artificial rain which symbolises life. Both the firewall and the back of the wax modules have mirrors installed to create the impression of a complex space that extends into the infinite.

Circle of Life

Focusing on the senses, the genetic code is a spatial installation. During the day the media content displays a magical metaphorical language with the images focusing on the circle of life. The installation thus creates a living image of Serono as a leading company in the area of biotechnology.

The choreography of the videos is based on the course of a single day and depicts different stages of life that correspond to the current time – starting with a single cell (early in the morning) right through to a mature adult (late in the evening). The basic display consists of atmospheric, abstract video clips. Whenever a person crosses the bridge, a motion detector causes the integrated LEDs to display a thematically linked image. Real images such as a baby or a pregnant woman – both stages in the "Circle of Life" – are superimposed upon the abstract area: people entering the foyer start interacting with the installation.

Serono gehört zu den weltweit führenden Pharmaunternehmen im Bereich der Biotechnologie und erweitert sein Headquarter in Genf.

Der architektonische Entwurf von Helmut Jahn integriert das bereits vorhandene, alte Gebäude in die neue Unternehmenszentrale. Eine Brandwand des bestehenden Gebäudes wird zur Rückseite eines Atriums, das Teil eines neuen, repräsentativen Eingangsbereichs ist.

Helmut Jahn bat ag4 mediatecture company® um ein Konzept, das die inhaltliche Ausrichtung von Serono im Bereich der Brandwand mediatektonisch inszeniert.

Layers of Life

ag4 kreierte eine Rauminstallation, die aus einer Schichtung unterschiedlicher Layer besteht. Module aus reinem Bienenwachs versinnbildlichen als Layer den genetischen Code. In die Wachsmodule ist eine Schicht Leuchtdioden integriert. Dieser Layer ermöglicht die mediale Bespielung der Installation. Zwischen der Brandwand und der Ebene der Wachselemente repräsentiert künstlicher Regen Wasser als Symbol des Lebens. Die Brandwand sowie die Rückseite der Wachsmodule sind verspiegelt und erzeugen den Eindruck eines komplexen, sich ins Unendliche erstreckenden Raums.

Circle of Life

Der genetische Code wird als Rauminstallation sinnlich inszeniert. Während des Tages wird die Installation durch eine magische Bildsprache medial bespielt. Die Bilder thematisieren den Zyklus des Lebens. So erzeugt die Installation ein lebendiges Bild von Serono als führendes Unternehmen im Bereich der Biotechnologie.

Die Choreographie der Videos orientiert sich am Tagesverlauf und zeigt entsprechend der Tageszeit verschiedene Stadien des Lebens – von der Zelle (früh am Morgen) bis zum erwachsenen Menschen (spät abends). Die Basisbespielung besteht aus atmosphärischen, abstrakten Videoclips. Wenn eine Person die Brücke betritt, wird über einen Bewegungsmelder ein Impuls ausgelöst, der die integrierte LED-Fläche thematisch zum Blühen bringt. Reale Bildelemente, wie z.B. ein Baby oder eine schwangere Frau – als Stadien des "Circle of Life" – überlagern dann die abstrakte Fläche: die Personen im Raum treten mit der Installation in Interaktion.

Serono, l'une des plus grandes entreprises pharmaceutiques de biotechnologie au monde, est en train d'agrandir son siège à Genève.

Le concept architectonique proposé par Helmut Jahn intègre les anciens bâtiments existants au nouveau siège de l'entreprise. L'un des murs coupe-feu de l'ancien bâtiment est transformé en façade arrière d'un atrium du nouveau hall d'entrée, qui a une fonction de représentation.

Helmut Jahn a chargé ag4 mediatecture company® de réaliser dans la zone du mur coupe-feu un concept de mise en scène médiatectonique de l'orientation de l'entreprise Serono.

Plaines de la vie

ag4 a mis au point une installation intérieure composée d'une superposition de différentes couches. Des modules en pure cire d'abeille symbolisent le code génétique sous forme de couches. Une couche de diodes lumineuses intégrée aux modules de cire permet la mise en scène médiatique de l'installation. Entre le mur coupe-feu et les éléments en cire, une pluie artificielle met en scène l'eau comme le symbole de la vie. Le mur coupe-feu et la façade arrière des modules en cire sont recouverts de miroirs et donnent aux visiteurs l'impression qu'ils se trouvent dans un espace complexe et infini.

Le circuit de la vie

Grâce à cette installation intérieure, le code génétique est mis en scène avec volupté. Dans la journée, l'installation sert de support à la mise en scène d'un langage visuel magique. Les images diffusées s'articulent autour du thème du cycle de la vie. Ainsi, l'installation diffuse une image vivante de Serono, entreprise de pointe dans le secteur de la biotechnologie.

La chorégraphie des vidéos se déroule parallèlement à l'évolution de la journée et montre différents stades de la vie en fonction de l'heure qu'il est – de la cellule (tôt le matin) à une personne adulte (tard le soir). La mise en scène de base est composée de vidéo-clips d'ambiance abstraits. Dès qu'une personne pose le pied sur la passerelle, un capteur de mouvements déclenche une impulsion qui provoque l'apparition de fleurs sur le panneau DEL. Ensuite, cette surface abstraite est peu à peu remplacée par des images réelles – un bébé, une femme enceinte – qui représentent différents « cycles de vie » : les personnes qui se trouvent dans la pièce interagissent avec l'installation.

Serono es una de las empresas farmacéuticas líder mundial en el ámbito de la biotecnología y está ampliando su sede central en Ginebra.

El proyecto arquitectónico de Helmut Jahn integra el edificio ya existente en la nueva sede de la empresa. Un cortafuegos del edificio antiguo será la zona posterior de un atrio que forma parte de un nuevo vestíbulo representativo.

Helmut Jahn solicitó a ag4 mediatecture company® un concepto para representar mediatectónicamente en el ámbito del cortafuegos la orientación conceptual de Serono.

Estratos de vida

ag4 concibió una instalación espacial que consiste en una superposición de estratos. Módulos de cera pura de abejas simbolizan estratificados el código genético. En los módulos de cera hay una capa de diodos luminiscentes integrada, que hace posible una escenificación mediática de la instalación. Entre el cortafuegos y el nivel de los elementos de cera, una lluvia artificial representa el agua como símbolo de la vida. El cortafuegos y la parte posterior de los módulos de cera están recubiertos de espejos y producen la sensación de un espacio complejo que se prolonga hasta el infinito.

El ciclo de la vida

El código genético se representa de forma sensorial a modo de instalación espacial. Durante el día, la instalación se pone en escena mediáticamente a través de un mágico leguaje visual. Las imágenes giran en torno al ciclo de la vida. De ese modo, la instalación da una imagen viva de Serono como empresa líder en el campo de la biotecnología.

La coreografía de los vídeos se adapta al discurrir de la jornada y, en función de la hora del día, muestra estadios de la vida –desde la célula (por la mañana temprano) hasta el hombre adulto (al final de la tarde)–. Los contenidos de la escenificación básica comprenden vídeo clips atmosféricos y abstractos. Cuando una persona atraviesa el puente, un sensor de movimiento envía un impulso que hace que la superficie LED integrada florezca temáticamente. Imágenes reales, como por ejemplo un bebé o una mujer embarazada –como estadios del ciclo de la vida–, se superponen entonces a la superficie abstracta: las personas en la sala interactúan con la instalación.

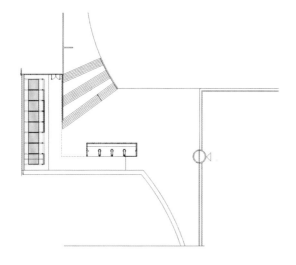

La Serono è una delle aziende farmaceutiche più importanti del mondo nel campo delle biotecnologie e sta ampliando la propria sede principale, a Ginevra.

Il progetto architettonico di Helmut Jahn integra gli edifici esistenti nel nuovo corpo centrale dell'azienda. Un muro spartifuoco dell'edificio esistente diventerà la parete di fondo di un atrio che è parte integrante di una nuova zona d'ingresso di rappresentanza.

Helmut Jahn ha richiesto alla ag4 mediatecture company® di sviluppare un progetto che metta in scena in senso mediatico-architettonico il nuovo orientamento contenutistico della Serono nell'area del muro spartifuoco.

Le Piane de la vita

ag4 ha creato a questo scopo un'installazione ambientale costituita da più strati sovrapposti (layers): moduli di pura cera d'api che simboleggiano gli strati del codice genetico. Nel modulo di cera è integrato uno strato di LED luminosi, che permette la messa in scena mediatica dell'installazione. Tra il muro spartifuoco e il piano degli elementi di cera, una pioggia artificiale rappresenta l'acqua come simbolo della vita. Il muro spartifuoco e la parte posteriore dei moduli sono rivestiti di specchi e creano l'impressione di un ambiente complesso, che si estende all'infinito.

Il circolo de la vita

Il codice genetico viene messo in scena come installazione ambientale e percepito in maniera sensoriale. Nel corso della giornata, l'installazione viene animata attraverso uno speciale linguaggio per immagini, che tematizzano il ciclo della vita, con una magia tutta particolare. In questo senso, l'installazione crea un quadro vivente della Serono come azienda di primaria importanza nel campo delle biotecnologie.

La coreografia dei video è orientata in base allo scorrere delle ore del giorno e mostra, in relazione al momento della giornata, le diverse fasi della vita: dalla singola cellula (al mattino presto) fino alla persona nell'età adulta (la sera tardi). La messa in scena di base è costituita da videoclip astratti o filmati di eventi atmosferici. Quando una persona passa sul ponte, tramite un sensore di movimento viene trasmesso un impulso che fa illuminare a tema la superficie a LED integrata. Elementi visivi reali, ad esempio un neonato o una donna incinta – in quanto stadi di questo "Circle of Life" – si sovrappongono alla superficie astratta: le persone presenti nell'ambiente interagiscono con l'installazione.

GLOBE
START AMADEUS | BAD HOMBURG
Realisation: 2000

In 1999 Start Amadeus (today Amadeus GmbH) built the new company headquarters in Bad Homburg. Start Amadeus is a company that specialises in the development and maintenance of administration systems for the tourism industry.

The management board was looking for a special site that would reflect Start Amadeus' identity. ag4 developed a space filling, media tectonical installation in the foyer – the foyer as a house within a house.

A cube made from aluminium panels covered with thin wooden veneer is illuminated by an aura of light whose origin is somewhat elusive. Specially developed floodlights made of LEDs provide the room with a variety of differently coloured schemes. These schemes can be controlled interactively by turning a globe positioned in the middle of the room.

More than 100,000 LEDs project the image of the earth onto the frosted glass surface of a globe. The terrestrial sphere is depicted using a climatic chart which subdivides the world into differently coloured zones. According to the selected zone the whole colour scheme of the cube and therefore the light aura in the foyer changes. In this way the visitor travels around the world while controlling the atmosphere of the space. There are many marked places to access which are linked to a pool of information. By touching the globe this information is displayed on a plasma display.

1999 baute Start Amadeus (heutige Amadeus GmbH) eine neue Firmenzentrale in Bad Homburg. Start Amadeus ist ein Unternehmen, das Buchungssysteme für die Touristikbranche entwickelt und betreut.

Die Geschäftsleitung suchte nach einem besonderen Ort, der die Identität von Start Amadeus verkörpert. ag4 entwickelte eine raumfüllende, mediatektonische Installation im Foyer – das Foyer als Haus im Haus.

Ein Kubus aus dünnen, mit Holzfurnier laminierten Aluminium-Panelen wird durch eine Lichtaura illuminiert, deren Ursprung im Verborgenen liegt. Speziell entwickelte Lichtfluter aus Leuchtdioden tauchen den Raum in verschiedene Farbstimmungen.Die Farbstimmungen können durch das Drehen eines Globus von der Mitte des Raumes aus interaktiv gesteuert werden.

Über 100.000 Leuchtdioden projizieren das Bild der Weltkugel auf die mattierte Glasschale des Globus. Die Weltkugel wird mittels einer Klimakarte dargestellt, die die Welt in verschiedene Farbzonen unterteilt. Entsprechend der angesteuerten Klimazone ändert sich der Farbton der Lichtaura im Foyer. So reist der Besucher um die Welt und steuert gleichzeitig die Atmosphäre des Raumes. Auf der Weltkugel können viele markierte Orte angesteuert werden. Sie sind mit einem Pool von Informationen über den Ort verlinkt, die bei Berührung der Kugel auf einem Plasmabildschirm aufgerufen werden.

En 1999, l'entreprise Start Amadeus (aujourd'hui Amadeus GmbH) a fait construire un nouveau siège d'entreprise à Bad Homburg. Start Amadeus est spécialisé dans le développement et le suivi de systèmes de réservation pour le secteur touristique.

La direction de l'entreprise était à la recherche d'un lieu particulier pour incarner l'identité de Start Amadeus. Dans le foyer, ag4 a imaginé une installation médiatectonique mettant en scène le foyer comme une maison dans la maison.

Un cube, composé de panneaux d'aluminium plaqués de bois, est éclairé par une aura lumineuse dont l'origine reste cachée. Des projecteurs à DEL spécialement conçus pour ce projet plongent la pièce dans différentes atmosphères colorées. En tournant un globe situé au centre de la pièce, on peut interagir avec l'installation et modifier les atmosphères colorées.

Plus de cent mille DEL projettent l'image du globe terrestre sur le verre dépoli du globe. Le globe terrestre est représenté sur la base d'une carte climatique divisant le monde en différentes zones colorées. Les nuances de l'aura lumineuse du foyer changent en fonction de la zone climatique vers laquelle on se dirige. Ainsi, le visiteur fait le tour du monde tout en contrôlant l'atmosphère de la pièce. On peut se diriger vers de nombreux sites mis en évidence sur le globe terrestre. Ils sont reliés à un système d'informations relatives au lieu sélectionné et qui s'affichent automatiquement sur un écran plasma lorsqu'on touche le globe.

En 1999, Start Amadeus (hoy Amadeus GmbH), una empresa que desarrolla y gestiona sistemas de reservas para el sector turístico, construyó una nueva sede central en Bad Homburg.

La dirección de la empresa buscó un lugar especial que personificara la identidad de Start Amadeus. ag4 desarrolló una instalación mediatectónica para el espacio del vestíbulo - el vestíbulo a modo de casa en la casa.

Un cubo de finos paneles laminados de aluminio chapados en madera es iluminado por una aureola de luz cuyo origen está oculto. Cuadros lumínicos de diodos luminiscentes ideados a tal fin sumergen el espacio en distintas tonalidades. Los matices de color pueden modificarse interactivamente girando el globo situado en el centro de la sala.

Más de 100.000 diodos luminiscentes proyectan la imagen de la esfera terráquea sobre la superficie de cristal mate del globo. La bola del mundo está representada en el centro de un mapa climático que divide el mundo en zonas de colores distintos. Según la zona climática a la que se oriente, cambia el tono de color de la aureola de luz en el vestíbulo. De ese modo, el visitante viaja alrededor de la Tierra y al mismo tiempo controla la atmósfera de la estancia. En el globo terráqueo hay muchos puntos marcados por los que se puede navegar. Están enlazados con un pool de informaciones sobre el lugar que, al tocar la bola, aparece en una pantalla de plasma.

Nel 1999 Start Amadeus (oggi solo Amadeus GmbH) ha costruito una nuova sede a Bad Homburg. Start Amadeus è un'azienda che si occupa dello sviluppo e dell'assistenza di sistemi di prenotazione per il settore turistico.

La direzione cercava un luogo particolare, che in qualche modo rispecchiasse l'identità di Start Amadeus. ag4 ha progettato un'installazione mediatica/architettonica nel foyer, grande quanto tutto il locale − il foyer come casa all'interno della casa.

Un cubo costituito da sottili pannelli d'alluminio laminato in legno viene illuminato da un'aura luminosa, la cui fonte è nascosta. Onde di luce, sviluppate appositamente e provenienti dai LED, immergono l'ambiente in sfumature di colore sempre diverse. I colori della luce possono essere cambiati anche in modo interattivo, semplicemente ruotando il globo che si trova al centro del locale.

Più di 100.000 LED proiettano l'immagine del globo terrestre sulla cupola in vetro satinato del Globus. Il globo terrestre viene rappresentato da una carta climatica, che suddivide il mondo in diverse zone di colore. In base alla zona climatica prescelta, il tono di colore dell'aura luminosa nel foyer cambia. Il visitatore compie così un viaggio virtuale attorno al mondo e allo stesso tempo interviene sull'atmosfera dell'ambiente. Sul globo terrestre si possono raggiungere diversi punti segnalati, i quali sono collegati con un pool di informazioni sul luogo prescelto, che può essere richiamato semplicemente sfiorando lo schermo al plasma che si trova sulla parete di fronte.

AUTOACTIVE PROGRAMMING

AUTOAKTIVE BESPIELUNG

LA MISE EN SCÈNE AUTO-ACTIVE

ESCENIFICACIÓN AUTOACTIVA

MESSA IN SCENA AUTOATTIVA

Targeted communication of current events

Autoactive programming consists of classic imagery and video material as well as animated texts and graphics. A modular content management system which can be designed to precisely meet individual client's needs is responsible for managing the autoactive display. It provides the medialised facade with targeted and always up-to-date content without the need for intensive editorial supervision.

Autoactive programming is especially suited for information, brand communication and emotional imagery. It fully realises its potential as communicative accompaniment and as (live) coverage of events.

Because of the limited amount and length of images available repetition cannot be avoided. The content management system, however, organises the contents into small units which are presented in constantly changing combinations or integrates them into an interactive or a reactive background display.

Zielgerichtete Kommunikation aktueller Ereignisse

Autoaktive Bespielungen bestehen aus klassischem Bild- und Videomaterial sowie animierten Texten und Grafiken. Das Bespielungsmaterial wird über ein Content-Management-System verwaltet, das als Baukastensystem individuell auf die Anforderungen des Kunden zugeschnitten ist. Es ermöglicht ohne großen redaktionellen Aufwand eine zielgerichtete und tagesaktuelle Bespielung der Medienfassade.

Die autoaktive Bespielung eignet sich besonders gut für Information, Markenkommunikation und emotionale Bilddarstellungen. Als kommunikative Begleitung und (Live-)Dokumentation von Veranstaltungen entfaltet sie ihr volles Potential.

Da die begrenzte Anzahl und Länge des Bildmaterials zu einer schnellen Wiederholung der Inhalte führt, ist es wichtig, sie mit Hilfe des Content-Management-Systems als kleine Einheiten in immer neuen Kombinationen zu präsentieren bzw. die autoaktive Bespielung in die Basisbespielung einer interaktiven oder reaktiven Bespielung zu integrieren.

Communication ciblée d'événements d'actualité

Les mises en scène auto-actives se composent d'images et de ressources vidéo classiques ainsi que de textes et d'images animés. Les ressources diffusées sont gérées par un système de gestion des contenus. Il s'agit là d'un système modulaire conçu sur mesure, capable de répondre aux exigences spécifiques du client. La façade médiatique présente ainsi une mise en scène ciblée et actualisée au quotidien, ne nécessitant pas de grands travaux rédactionnels.

La mise en scène auto-active est idéale pour diffuser des informations, une image de marque ou encore des représentations graphiques émotionnelles. Elle montre tout son potentiel notamment quand il s'agit de communiquer et de documenter des manifestations en direct.

Le nombre limité et la durée restreinte des images entraînant une répétition rapide du contenu, il est important de renouveler sans cesse les combinaisons d'images à l'aide du système de gestion des contenus sous forme de petites unités, et d'intégrer la mise en scène auto-active à la diffusion de base d'une mise en scène interactive ou réactive.

Comunicación concreta de acontecimientos actuales

Las escenificaciones autoactivas combinan material visual y de vídeo clásico con un contingente gráfico y textual. Los contenidos presentados se gestionan por un administrador de contenido (Content Management System) que, como un sistema de unidades de módulos, se adapta a las necesidades de los clientes. Ello permite que la escenificación de la fachada mediática pueda tener un objetivo claro y plena actualidad sin grandes costes redaccionales.

La presentación autoactiva resulta especialmente indicada para la trasmisión de información, la difusión de marcas y las presentaciones emocionales de imágenes. Su mayor potencial se despliega en el ámbito del acompañamiento comunicativo y la documentación (en directo) de actos diversos.

Dado que la limitada cantidad y duración del material visual hacen inevitable una rápida repetición de los contenidos, es importante que, con ayuda del sistema administrador de contenido, se presenten en pequeñas unidades siempre en nuevas combinaciones o que la escenificación autoactiva se integre en el programa de base de una puesta en escena interactiva o reactiva.

Comunicazione mirata di eventi attuali

Una messa in scena autoattiva è costituita da materiale visivo classico e video, nonché da testi animati e grafica. Il materiale per la messa in scena viene gestito tramite un Content Management System, confezionato su misura per le necessità del cliente, un po' come un gioco di costruzioni. In questo modo si realizza una messa in scena mirata e sempre aggiornata della facciata mediatica, eliminando il costoso apparato di redazione.

La messa in scena autoattiva è particolarmente adatta per l'informazione, comunicazioni sul marchio e rappresentazioni di immagini che vanno a toccare le emozioni. Come accompagnamento comunicativo e documentazione (anche live) di eventi e manifestazioni sviluppa in pieno il suo potenziale.

Poiché, dato il numero e la durata del materiale visivo piuttosto limitati, si ha una rapida ripetizione dei contenuti, con l'aiuto del Content Management System è importante presentarli come piccole unità in combinazioni sempre diverse, oppure integrare la messa in scena autoattiva nel materiale di base di una messa in scena interattiva o reattiva.

WINDOW
GALERIA KAUFHOF | ALEXANDERPLATZ BERLIN
Concept: 2005
Architects: Kleihues + Kleihues

As part of a general refurbishment, the department store Galeria Kaufhof on the Alexanderplatz in Berlin is planning the integration of a media facade into the new natural stone facade. ag4 proposes a transparent media facade placed in front of the extensive windows. Contrary to a normal proprietary LED video display which was to be placed in front of the natural stone facade akin to a stamp, the media facade merges with the building and because of its size fits in perfectly with the surrounding architecture of the Alexanderplatz.

The media facade enables Galeria Kaufhof to medially stage its brand not only on its building but also on a prominent site within the city. Furthermore, it can be used as a large catwalk for fashion and product shows. The media facade also pays tribute to the urbanity of the Alexanderplatz as it will broadcast large scale events such as the Soccer World Cup in 2006. Back in everyday life the transparent media facade broadcasts events happening inside the building to the outside. In practice this means that cameras capture the central glass escalator including shoppers and display everything as auto-active live event on the facade.

Galeria Kaufhof am Alexanderplatz in Berlin plant im Rahmen eines Umbaus die Integration einer Medienfläche in die neue Natursteinfassade. ag4 schlägt eine Transparente Medienfassade vor, die den großflächigen Fenstern vorgelagert wird. Entgegen einem handelsüblichen LED-Videoboard, das ähnlich einer Briefmarke vor die Natursteinfassade gesetzt werden sollte, verschmilzt die Medienfassade mit der Architektur und passt sich durch ihre Größe dem städtebaulichen Maßstab des Alexanderplatz' an.

Mit der Medienfassade kann Galeria Kaufhof seine Marke am eigenen Gebäude und gleichzeitig an einem prominenten Platz in der Stadt medial inszenieren. Weiterhin kann sie als großer Catwalk für Mode- und Produktschauen genutzt werden. Der Urbanität des Alexanderplatz' wird sie gerecht, indem Großveranstaltungen wie die Fußball WM 2006 live auf der Fassade übertragen werden. Im Alltag kehrt die Transparente Medienfassade das Geschehen im Inneren des Gebäudes nach Außen und Kameras spielen die zentrale gläserne Rolltreppe des Gebäudes mit ihrem Publikumsverkehr als autoaktives Live-Ereignis auf die Fassade.

Dans le cadre de sa reconstruction, la grande surface Galeria Kaufhof de l'Alexanderplatz de Berlin envisage d'intégrer une surface médiatique à sa nouvelle façade en pierre naturelle. ag4 propose une façade médiatique transparente placée devant les vastes fenêtres. Contrairement à un écran vidéo à DEL traditionnel, qui serait posé devant la façade en pierre naturelle comme un timbre, la façade médiatique fusionne avec l'architecture et s'adapte parfaitement, grâce à sa taille, à la mesure urbanistique de l'Alexanderplatz.

La façade médiatique permet à Galeria Kaufhof de mettre sa marque en scène d'une part sur son propre bâtiment, et d'autre part sur l'une des grandes places de la ville. De plus, elle peut servir de podium pour les défilés de mode et présentations de produits. La façade médiatique satisfait à l'urbanité de la place Alexanderplatz dans la mesure où il est possible d'y retransmettre en direct de grandes manifestations comme la Coupe du Monde de Football en 2006. Au quotidien, la façade médiatique transparente expose au monde extérieur ce qui se passe à l'intérieur du bâtiment ; des caméras enregistrent puis diffusent sur la façade, sous forme de mise en scène auto-active en direct, un film montrant l'escalier roulant transparent situé au centre du bâtiment, avec les allées et venues du public.

En el marco de una remodelación de su inmueble, Galeria Kaufhof (unos grandes almacenes) de la Alexanderplatz de Berlín planea la integración de una fachada mediática en la nueva fachada de piedra natural. La propuesta de ag4 consiste en una fachada mediática transparente que se instala delante de los grandes escaparates. A diferencia de un panel LED de vídeo tradicional que iba a colocarse a modo de sello delante de la fachada de piedra natural, la fachada mediática se funde con la arquitectura y se ajusta por su tamaño a la normativa urbanística prescrita para la Alexanderplatz.

Con la fachada propuesta por ag4, Galeria Kaufhof puede escenificar mediáticamente su marca comercial en el propio edificio y al mismo tiempo en una concurrida plaza de la ciudad. Además, puede emplearse como gran pasarela para exhibiciones de moda u otros productos. El edificio se pone a la altura de la urbanidad de la Alexanderplatz, trasmitiendo en directo desde su fachada eventos importantes, tales como el Campeonato Mundial de Fútbol de 2006. En el discurrir cotidiano, la fachada mediática transparente lleva al exterior lo que sucede en el interior, y unas cámaras proyectan en la fachada la escalera mecánica central de cristal del edificio con su trasiego de gente como suceso autoactivo en directo.

Per Galeria Kaufhof, grande centro commerciale nella centrale Alexanderplatz, a Berlino, nel contesto di una ristrutturazione si decide l'integrazione di una superficie mediatica nella nuova facciata in pietra naturale. ag4 propone una facciata mediatica trasparente, posta davanti alle ampie vetrate. Anziché un normale schermo commerciale a LED, che avrebbe dato l'impressione di un francobollo attaccato alla facciata in pietra, la facciata mediatica si fonde con l'architettura e si adatta per grandezza alla dimensione urbanistica della Alexanderplatz.

Con la facciata mediatica, Galeria Kaufhof riesce a mettere in scena in modo mediale il marchio sulla propria sede e allo stesso tempo in un luogo rappresentativo della città. Inoltre può essere utilizzata come gigantesca passerella per sfilate di moda e presentazione di prodotti. Viene anche conservata l'osmosi con la piazza; ad esempio, grandi eventi come i Mondiali di calcio del 2006 verranno trasmessi in diretta sulla facciata. Nella vita quotidiana del centro commerciale, la facciata mediatica trasparente porta all'esterno quanto accade all'interno dell'edificio, con filmati della scala mobile interna e il suo traffico di pubblico, proiettati sulla facciata come eventi *live* autoattivi.

ag4 mediatecture company® developed a concept for the LTU-Arena on the river Rhine in Dusseldorf which envisaged the medialisation of the side of the stadium that faces the parking lot.

The LTU-Arena facade consists of pipes that have been placed in front of a glass facade and act as a sunscreen. This side facing the Rhine is to be adapted to include a transparent media facade with LEDs integrated into the pipes. The resulting facade will have two areas with different resolutions. The area with the higher resolution is capable of displaying video content. From a distance of more than 100 metres one can watch advertisements as well as live images from inside the stadium that are inserted into the normal media programme. The part of the media facade with a lower resolution is reserved for the depiction of charts, writing and coloured visualisations. The combination of these two different resolutions enables the medialisation of an area of 6,000 square metres on a low budget.

Für die LTU-Arena am Rhein in Düsseldorf entwickelte ag4 mediatecture company® ein Konzept, um die dem Parkplatz zugewandte Seite des Stadions zu medialisieren.

Die Fassade der LTU-Arena besteht aus Rohren, die als Sonnenschutz vor die Glasfassade gehängt werden. Diese Fassade wird zur Rheinseite hin zu einer Transparenten Medienfassade umgebaut, indem LEDs in die Rohre integriert werden. In dieser Medienfassade gibt es zwei Bereiche mit unterschiedlicher Auflösung. Der Bereich mit der höheren Auflösung ist videofähig. Bei einem Betrachtungsabstand ab 100 Metern können hier Werbeclips und Live-Bilder aus dem Stadion in die Bespielung einfließen. Der Teil der Medienfassade mit einer geringeren Auflösung ermöglicht die Darstellung von Grafik, Schrift und Farbatmosphären. Die Kombination dieser beiden unterschiedlichen Auflösungen ermöglicht es, eine Fläche von 6.000 Quadratmetern auch mit einem geringeren Budget zu medialisieren.

Pour le LTU-Arena de Düsseldorf, sur le Rhin, ag4 mediatecture company®, a mis au point un concept permettant de mettre en scène l'aile du stade tournée vers le parking.

Des tuyaux sont accrochés devant la façade en verre du LTU-Arena pour la protéger du soleil. Vers le Rhin, cette façade est transformée en façade médiatique transparente en intégrant des DEL aux tuyaux. La façade médiatique est divisée en deux parties distinctes aux résolutions différentes. La partie à haute résolution peut retransmettre des vidéos. A partir d'une distance d'observation de 100 mètres, on peut y faire défiler des films publicitaires ou des images en direct du stade. La partie de la façade médiatique dont la résolution est la moins élevée permet la diffusion d'images, de messages ou d'atmosphères colorées. La combinaison de ces deux résolutions différentes permet de mettre en scène une surface de 6 000 mètres carrés malgré un budget réduit.

Para el estadio LTU Arena a orillas del Rin en Düsseldorf, ag4 mediatecture company®, desarrolló un concepto mediático para la fachada orientada al aparcamiento.

La fachada del LTU Arena consta de tubos que, a modo de parasol, están colocados delante de la fachada de cristal. Esa fachada, en la cara orientada al Rin, se transforma en una fachada mediática integrando LEDs en los tubos. En esta fachada mediática hay dos ámbitos con resoluciones diferentes. La zona de mayor resolución es apta para vídeo, y puede mostrar spots publicitarios e imágenes en directo del estadio para ser observados a partir de una distancia de 100 metros. La zona de la fachada mediática con menor resolución permite la presentación de material gráfico, texto y atmósferas tonales. Con la combinación de estas dos resoluciones distintas se consigue la mediatización de una superficie de 6.000 metros cuadrados con un presupuesto modesto.

Per la LTU Arena sul Reno, a Düsseldorf, ag4 mediatecture company® ha presentato un progetto per medializzare il lato dello stadio orientato verso l'area parcheggio.

La facciata della LTU Arena è costituita da tubi metallici frangisole sospesi davanti alla facciata in vetro. Dalla parte che guarda verso il Reno questa facciata è stata trasformata in facciata mediatica trasparente, integrando i LED all'interno dei tubi. In questa facciata mediatica vi sono due zone con risoluzioni diverse. La zona a risoluzione più alta è predisposta per i video. A una distanza di osservazione di 100 metri si possono essere mostrare clip pubblicitarie e filmati live dall'interno dello stadio. La zona di facciata a risoluzione minore consente di esporre grafiche, scritte e giochi di luce e colore. La combinazione delle due zone a diversa risoluzione permette di medializzare una superficie di 6000 metri quadrati anche con un budget relativamente ridotto.

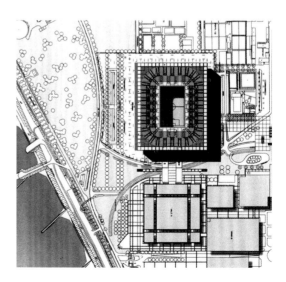

SPIRIT
MEDIA PORT | DUSSELDORF
Concept: 2001
Architect: Helmut Jahn

In 2002 Helmut Jahn was commissioned to plan an office block for the Media Port in Dusseldorf. In cooperation with ag4 mediatecture company®, Helmut Jahn developed a succinct medialisation which was to elevate the building to becoming the landmark of the Media Port.

The gill-like overlapping glass plates which serve to air the building lend it a special character. They are arranged in horizontal bars and are thus ideally suited for an economically efficient medialisation of the entire building. In order to underline the architectural clarity and elegance in form, the media programme is restricted to monochrome displays in white and green.

The basic imagery are organic visualisations which provide the building with magical poetic dynamics. However, the horizontal strands are also broad enough to be able to display large scale text.

2002 erhielt Helmut Jahn den Auftrag, ein Bürohochhaus für den Düsseldorfer Medienhafen zu planen. Gemeinsam mit ag4 mediatecture company®, entwickelte Helmut Jahn eine prägnante Medialisierung, die das Gebäude zum Wahrzeichen des Medienhafen werden lassen sollte.

Die kiemenartig überlappenden Glasschotten, die der Belüftung des Gebäudes dienen, geben ihm seinen besonderen Charakter. Durch ihre horizontale Streifenanordnung eignen sie sich sehr gut für eine kostengünstige Komplettmedialisierung des Gebäudes. Um die Architektur in ihrer Klarheit und Eleganz zu unterstützen, ist die mediale Bespielung monochrom in weiß und grün gehalten.

Basisbespielung sind organisch verlaufende Strukturen, die dem Gebäude eine magisch-poetische Dynamik verleihen. Die horizontalen Bänder sind jedoch auch breit genug, um weithin sichtbar Text darzustellen.

En 2002, Helmut Jahn a été chargé d'imaginer un immeuble de bureaux pour le Medienhafen de Düsseldorf. La remarquable mise en scène médiatique du bâtiment, réalisée par Helmut Jahn en collaboration avec ag4 mediatecture company®, était amenée à transformer le bâtiment en emblème du Medienhafen.

Les cloisons d'aération en verre du bâtiment, qui font penser à des branchies, confèrent au tour son caractère particulier. Leur alignement horizontal se prête parfaitement à une mise en scène médiatique de l'ensemble du bâtiment à moindres frais. Afin de souligner la clarté et l'élégance de l'architecture, la mise en scène médiatique est monochrome, en vert et blanc.

La diffusion de base représente un déroulement continu de structures organiques qui donnent au bâtiment un dynamisme magique et poétique. Mais les bandes horizontales sont également assez larges pour y faire défiler des messages lisibles de loin.

Helmut Jahn recibió en 2002 el encargo de proyectar un edificio de oficinas para el Medienhafen (antiguo puerto fluvial donde tienen su sede actualmente diversos medios de comunicación) de Düsseldorf. Junto con ag4 mediatecture company®, Jahn concibió una precisa mediatización que tenía como objeto convertir el edificio en un emblema del Medienhafen.

Las particiones de vidrio superpuestas a modo de branquias, que tienen como finalidad favorecer la ventilación del edificio, le confieren su carácter singular. Dada su disposición en bandas horizontales, resultan óptimas para una completa mediatización del edificio sin demasiados costes. Para fomentar la claridad y la elegancia de la arquitectura, se ha optado por una escenificación monocromática en blanco y en verde.

La escenificación de base se compone de estructuras orgánicas que van difuminándose y que proporcionan al edificio una dinámica mágico-poética. Las bandas horizontales son además lo suficientemente anchas como para permitir mostrar texto legible a gran distancia.

Nel 2002 Helmut Jahn ha ricevuto l'incarico di progettare un palazzo di uffici per il Mediaport di Düsseldorf. In collaborazione con ag4 mediatecture company®, Helmut Jahn ha sviluppato una medializzazione rappresentativa, che fa del grattacielo il simbolo del Mediaport.

Le paratie in vetro, sovrapposte come lamelle, che servono all'aerazione dell'edificio, ne definiscono anche il particolare carattere. Essendo disposte a fasce orizzontali, si sono dimostrate molto adatte a una medializzazione completa e a basso costo di tutto l'edificio. Per valorizzarne l'architettura in tutta la sua eleganza e leggerezza di linee, la messa in scena mediatica è mantenuta in due soli colori, il bianco e il verde.

Come messa in scena di base è stata data la preferenza a volumi fluttuanti in modo organico, che conferiscono all'edificio una dinamica sospesa tra magia e poesia. La fasce orizzontali sono tuttavia di larghezza sufficiente a mostrare testi leggibili da lontano.

INSIDE OUT
SRG TELEVISION STATION | BERN
Concept: 2004
Architects: Stücheli Architekten

As part of a competition for the conversion of a building belonging to the Swiss state television in Bern, ag4 media-tecture company® developed the medialisation for the Zurich architectural practice Stücheli. The initial design planned to furnish the entire facade with an external structure of vertical glass panels, part of which were to be medialised.

The edges of the glass panels have integrated LEDs. As sunscreens, the panels themselves are adjustable – a fact that enables a particularly attractive display at night by turning them by 180°. Now the LEDs illuminate the inside of the building and create an animated, coloured structure which can be seen from far away. This demonstrates the building's transparency especially at night.

The media programme during the day consists of an image which communicates the identity of Swiss television. A specific characteristic of Switzerland is that it has several official languages and therefore can also boast great cultural diversity. It is the task of Swiss television to communicate this fact in its programmes and it calls its method for doing so „Idee Swisse". The media programme thus includes a number of different animated texts in each of the official languages which overlap in a graphically artistic way and also start interacting – just like the Idee Swisse.

Im Rahmen eines Wettbewerbes für den Umbau des Gebäudes des Schweizer Staatsfernsehens in Bern entwickelte ag4 mediatecture company®, für das Zürcher Architekturbüro Stücheli die Medialisierung. Der Entwurf sah vor, die gesamte Gebäudefassade mit einer außenliegenden Struktur aus vertikalen Glaslamellen zu versehen. Teile der Fassade sollten medialisiert werden.

In die Kanten der Glaslamellen sind LEDs integriert. Die Lamellen sind drehbar und dienen als Sonnen-schutz. Dadurch bietet sich eine besondere Inszenierung des Gebäudes bei Nacht an, indem die Lamellen um 180° gedreht werden. So leuchten die LEDs in das Gebäude und ziehen eine animierte farbige Struktur auch von außen weit sicht-bar durch die Innenräume. Die Transparenz des Gebäudes wird nachts dadurch besonders herausgestellt.

Die Tagesbespielung kommuniziert ein Bild für die Identität des Schweizer Fernsehens. Eine Besonderheit der Schweiz ist ihre Multilingualität und damit auch ihre kulturelle Vielfalt. Das Schweizer Fernsehen hat die Aufgabe, diese in ihrem Programm zu vermitteln und nennt seine Methode dafür „Idee Swisse". In der Bespielung werden ver-schiedene Texte in den unterschiedlichen Landessprachen animiert. Sie überlagern sich grafisch-künstlerisch und treten miteinander in Interaktion – eben Idee Swisse.

Dans le cadre d'un concours d'idées organisé pour la transformation du bâtiment de la télévision publique suisse à Berne, ag4 mediatecture company®, a réalisé sa mise en scène médiatique pour le bureau d'architectes Stücheli. Le projet prévoyait d'équiper la totalité de la façade du bâtiment d'une structure extérieure composée de lamelles ver-ticales en verre. L'idée était de mettre en scène plusieurs parties de la façade.

Des DEL sont intégrées aux arêtes des lamelles de verre. Les lamelles sont mobiles et ont pour fonction initiale de protéger le bâtiment du soleil. En les faisant pivoter à 180 degrés, il est possible d'obtenir une mise en scène parti-culière du bâtiment la nuit. Ainsi, les DEL illuminent l'intérieur du bâtiment et traversent les pièces d'une structure colorée et animée visible de loin. De nuit, la transparence du bâtiment est ainsi particulièrement mise en valeur.

De jour, la mise en scène de base véhicule une image de l'identité de la télévision suisse. Une des particularités de la Suisse est son plurilinguisme et sa diversité culturelle. La télévision suisse, dont l'une des missions est de trans-mettre ces atouts grâce à ses programmes, appelle sa méthode « Idée suisse ». La diffusion est composée d'ani-mations de phrases rédigées dans les différentes langues du pays. Elles se superposent de manière artistique et interagissent les unes avec les autres – c'est l'esprit même de «l'Idée suisse».

En el ámbito de un concurso para la remodelación del edificio de la Emisora Estatal Suiza de Televisión (SRG) en Berna, ag4 mediatecture company®, concibió la mediatización para el despacho de arquitectos de Zúrich Stücheli. El proyecto preveía dotar todo el exterior de la fachada del edificio con una estructura de láminas de vidrio vertica-les. La mediatización estaba planeada para algunas zonas de la fachada.

Los cantos de las láminas de vidrio llevan LEDs integrados. Las láminas son giratorias y sirven de protección contra los rayos solares. Ello permite que durante la noche, girándolas 180°, el edificio muestre una particular escenificación. Al girar las láminas, los LEDs iluminan el edificio y proyectan una estructura de color animada por el espacio interior que resulta también visible a una gran distancia desde el exterior. De ese modo, por la noche se pone especialmente de relieve la transparencia del edificio.

Durante el día, la puesta en escena comunica una imagen representativa de la identidad de la televisión suiza. Una particularidad de Suiza es el multilinguismo y, unido a él, también la diversidad cultural. La televisión suiza tiene la tarea de fomentar dicha diversidad en su programación, y ha designado con el nombre de "Idee Swisse" al método que emplea para ello. En la puesta en escena mediática aparecen textos en las diferentes lenguas del país, dotados de movimiento, que se solapan unos a otros gráfica y artísticamente y que interaccionan unos con otros. He ahí la Idee Swisse.

Nell'ambito di un concorso per la ristrutturazione della sede della TV pubblica svizzera, a Berna, ag4 mediatecture company® ha realizzato la medializzazione per lo studio di architettura Stücheli di Zurigo. Il progetto prevedeva di rivestire l'intera facciata dell'edificio con una struttura esterna costituita da lamelle verticali in vetro. Parte della facciata doveva essere medializzata.

Negli spigoli delle lamelle sono integrati i LED. Le lamelle possono essere orientate e hanno funzione frangisole; ne deriva la possibilità di creare una particolare messa in scena nelle ore di buio, quando le lamelle sono ruotate di 180°. I LED illuminano l'edificio e rendono visibile da lontano anche dall'esterno una struttura animata dal colore attraverso lo spazio interno. La trasparenza dell'edificio viene così particolarmente evidenziata nelle ore notturne.

Durante il giorno, la messa in scena intende comunicare un'immagine per l'identità della televisione svizzera. Una particolarità della Svizzera è il plurilinguismo e quindi anche la molteplicità di culture. La televisione svizzera ha come missione la comunicazione di questo concetto attraverso i suoi programmi e denomina questo metodo Idee Swisse. Nella messa in scena vengono animati testi nelle diverse lingue ufficiali della Confederazione, che si sovrappongono l'uno all'altro in senso grafico e artistico ed entrano in interazione uno con l'altro – una Idee Swisse per immagini.

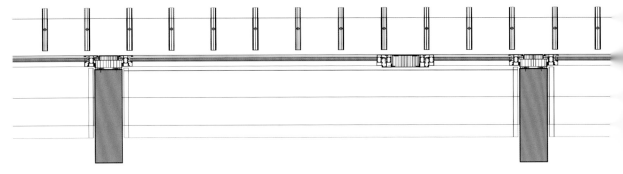

HYPERBOLOID
NISSAN SHOWROOM | DOHA
Concept: 2003
Architects: mangen + gerken GmbH

Medialisation of a car showroom in Doha should make the construction a real eye-catcher on an otherwise very busy road. The hyperboloid building has a facade with diagonal lines which are furnished with LEDs to enable proper media content.

During the day the mirror effect of the facade prevent the passer-by from being able to see inside. However, depicting the cars large scale onto the facade of the building serves as a real attention getter. In the evening the display depicts virtual windows which ideally medialise the illuminated cars inside the showroom.

Der Showroom eines Autohauses an einer viel befahrenen Straße in Doha sollte durch eine Medialisierung zu einem besonderen Blickfang werden. Die diagonalen Linien der Fassadenkonstruktion der hyperboloiden Gebäudeform wurden als Basis für eine mediale Bespielung mit LEDs bestückt.

Tagsüber können die Fahrzeuge im Showroom aufgrund der Spiegelungen in der Fassade kaum wahrgenommen werden. Indem sie großflächig auf die Gebäudehaut medialisiert werden, erhöht sich die Aufmerksamkeit jedoch enorm. Abends bildet die Bespielung virtuelle Fenster aus, die die dahinterliegenden illuminierten Autos im Showroom gezielt medialisieren.

Ce projet consistait à transformer le showroom d'un concessionnaire automobile implanté le long d'une route très passante de Doha en véritable pôle d'attraction en procédant à sa mise en scène médiatique. Les lignes diagonales de la structure de la façade du bâtiment hyperboloïde ont été équipées de DEL, servant ainsi de base à la mise en scène médiatique.

De jour, les véhicules du showroom sont difficilement discernables de l'extérieur en raison des nombreux reflets dans la façade. Cependant, leur représentation en grand format sur la surface extérieure du bâtiment permet d'accroître considérablement l'attention des passants. De nuit, des fenêtres virtuelles s'ouvrent sur la façade ; derrière ces fenêtres, les voitures éclairées du showroom sont mises en scène de façon ciblée.

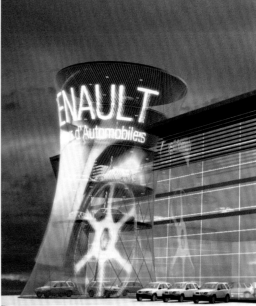

La sala de exposición de una empresa de automóviles situada en una calle con mucho tráfico de la ciudad de Doha debía convertirse en un punto de atracción especial con ayuda de una mediatización. La líneas diagonales de los elementos constructivos de la fachada del edificio, de planta hiperboloide, fueron dotados con LEDs como plataforma para una escenificación mediática.

Durante el día, los automóviles exhibidos en la sala de exposición pasaban casi desapercibidos por los numerosos reflejos en la fachada. En cambio, llevados en gran formato a la piel del edificio con ayuda mediática se llama considerablemente la atención. Por la noche, la puesta en escena proporciona escaparates virtuales que tienen como objetivo resaltar los automóviles que por detrás de ellos se muestran iluminados en la sala de exposición.

Lo showroom di una casa automobilistica che si affaccia su una strada di Doha molto trafficata è stato trasformato in un vero e proprio polo d'attrazione grazie a una medializzazione. Le linee oblique della facciata dell'edificio, che ha la forma di un iperboloide sono diventate la base per una messa in scena mediatica, una volta corredate di LED luminosi.

Durante il giorno, per la presenza della messa in scena sulla facciata, le autovetture che si trovano all'interno del salone vengono appena intraviste. Medializzandole in megaformato sulla superficie esterna dell'edificio, si attira enormemente l'attenzione. Nelle ore serali la messa in scena forma vetrine virtuali che mostrano, medializzate e in modo mirato, le auto che si trovano all'interno, adeguatamente illuminate.

As part of its 50th anniversary, McDonald's started an architectural competition for a flagship restaurant in Chicago. ag4 developed the medialisation concept for Helmut Jahn's architectural design.

Budget constraints limit the medialisation to the curved front of the upper level. Vertical segments are furnished with LEDs and attached at both ends of the media facade with steadily increasing gaps. This allows for a smooth change-over from a static to a medialised facade.

Jahn's design is pure pop art. Accordingly, the media display adds an additional ironic touch. Shrill, colourful tomatoes and cucumbers in pop art design chase one another, thus becoming the focus of attention.

Zu seinem 50-jährigen Jubiläum schrieb McDonald's für ein Flagship-Restaurant in Chicago einen Architektur-wettbewerb aus. ag4 entwickelte für den Entwurf von Helmut Jahn das Medialisierungskonzept.

Die Medialisierung beschränkt sich aus Kostengründen auf die gerundete Frontseite des Obergeschosses. Vertikale Lamellen werden mit LEDs bestückt und an den beiden Enden der Medienfassade in immer größeren Abständen montiert. Dies erlaubt einen weichen Übergang von der statischen zur medialisierten Fassade.

Der Entwurf von Jahn ist pure Pop Art. Entsprechend setzt die Bespielung einen zusätzlich ironischen Akzent. Schrille, bunte, im Pop Art-Stil gehaltene Tomaten und Gurken jagen sich gegenseitig und generieren Aufmerksam-keit.

A l'occasion de son cinquantième anniversaire, McDonald's a organisé un concours d'architecture pour un restaurant McDonald's de prestige à Chicago. ag4 a réalisé le concept de mise en scène médiatique pour le projet de Helmut Jahn.

Pour des raisons financières, la mise en scène médiatique se limite à la façade avant ronde de l'étage supérieur. Les lamelles verticales équipées de DEL qui composent la façade médiatique sont installées à intervalles de plus en plus espacés en se rapprochant des deux extrémités. Cela permet un passage en douceur de la façade statique à la façade médiatique.

Le projet de Jahn est du pur Pot Art. Corrélativement, la mise en scène médiatique lui confère un accent ironique supplémentaire : des tomates et des concombres tapageurs et bariolés de style Pop Art se poursuivent mutuellement et attirent ainsi l'attention des passants.

Con ocasión de su 50° aniversario, McDonald's convocó un concurso arquitectónico para la realización de un restaurante emblemático en Chicago. ag4 se encargó de desarrollar el concepto mediático para el proyecto de Helmut Jahn.

La mediatización se limita por cuestiones presupuestarias únicamente a la cara frontal circular de la planta superior. Láminas verticales se equipan con LEDs y se montan con una separación creciente a ambos extremos de la fachada mediática, para conseguir así que la transición entre la zona estática de la fachada y la mediatizada no resulte muy brusca.

El proyecto de Jahn es puro pop art y, en correspondencia, la puesta en escena añade una nota irónica: tomates y pepinos en el característico estilo estridente y colorista del pop art se dan caza mutuamente, generando un foco de atracción.

Per il suo cinquantesimo anniversario, McDonald's ha indetto un concorso per il disegno di un ristorante flagship a Chicago. ag4 ha realizzato la medializzazione per il progetto di Helmut Jahn.

Per ragioni economiche, la medializzazione è stata limitata alla parte frontale del piano superiore. I LED sono stati inseriti all'interno di lamelle verticali, montate più distanziate alle due estremità della facciata. In questo modo è possibile attuare il passaggio fluido da una situazione statica a una dinamica, medializzata, della facciata stessa.

Il progetto di Jahn è Pop Art pura. Adeguandosi, la messa in scena vuole sottolinearne ulteriormente l'aspetto ironico e divertente. Pomodori e cetrioli dai colori acidi, in perfetto stile Pop Art, si inseguono sulla facciata e catturano l'attenzione di chi passa.

REACTIVE PROGRAMMING

REAKTIVE BESPIELUNG

LA MISE EN SCÈNE RÉACTIVE

ESCENIFICACIÓN REACTIVA

MESSA IN SCENA REATTIVA

External parameters create an unlimited variety of images

Digital media enable a direct relationship between the content of a media facade and the events of the surrounding urban environment. The viewer can be addressed at precisely his or her point in space and time – for example standing in the rain. Cameras, sensors and modern software technology can gather external parameters in real time and convert the data into media content. The media facade thus reacts as if by magic to changes in its environment. Measurable factors include the weather, light or sounds but also quantitative data such as stock exchange prices or traffic congestion. The media facade thus turns into a permeable membrane which is not only subject to external factors on the outer layer of the building, but which reacts to and mirrors them in the form of media content. New real time technology stemming from the computer game industry enables the generation of constantly changing high quality images.

Contrary to the classic image medium of the film, reactive content is therefore not limited in time by a beginning and an end but recreates a new each and every second. The quality of the reactive content is defined by the choice of influencing factors as well as an adequate choreography of the generated images over a long time span. These qualities make reactive content an ideal base-display for media facades.

Externe Parameter erzeugen unendliche Bildervarianz

Die digitalen Medien ermöglichen es, bei der Bespielung einer Medienfassade unmittelbaren Bezug auf das Stadt- und Umweltgeschehen zu nehmen. Der Betrachter kann dort abgeholt werden, wo er sich gerade befindet – zum Beispiel im Regen. Mittels Kameras, Sensoren und moderner Softwaretechnologie können externe Parameter in Echtzeit erfasst und für die Bespielung genutzt werden. Die Medienfassade reagiert dann wie von Geisterhand gesteuert auf die Veränderungen in ihrer Umwelt. Messbare Einflussfaktoren sind beispielsweise das Wetter, die Lichtverhältnisse oder Geräusche der Umgebung, aber auch quantitative Daten wie z.B. Börsenkurse oder die Verkehrsdichte am Standort. Die Medienfassade wird so zu einer durchlässigen Membran, bei der externe Einflussfaktoren auf die Gebäudehaut wirken, von ihr aufgenommen und medial gespiegelt werden. Neue Echtzeittechnologien aus der Computerspielbranche ermöglichen es dabei, Bilder in ständiger Varianz zu generieren und in hoher Qualität darzustellen.

Im Gegensatz zum klassischen Bildmedium Film ist die reaktive Bespielung nicht mehr durch einen Anfang oder ein Ende zeitlich begrenzt, sondern erschafft sich in jeder Sekunde neu. Die Qualität der reaktiven Bespielung definiert sich durch die Wahl der Einflussfaktoren sowie eine adäquate Choreografie der generierten Bilder über einen langen Zeitraum. Damit eignet sich die reaktive Bespielung hervorragend zur Basisbespielung von Medienfassaden.

Des paramètres externes génèrent une variation infinie d'images

En mettant en scène la façade médiatique, les médias numériques se réfèrent directement à la vie dans la ville et aux événements locaux. Le spectateur peut être pris là où il se trouve en l'instant présent - par exemple sous la pluie. À l'aide de caméras, de capteurs et de technologies logicielles modernes, il est possible de saisir les paramètres externes en temps réel et de les exploiter pour la mise en scène. Comme animée par une main invisible, la façade médiatique réagit alors aux mutations de son environnement. Les facteurs mesurables sont par exemple la météo, la luminosité ou les bruits de l'environnement, mais aussi les données quantitatives telles que les cours de la Bourse ou la densité du trafic. La façade médiatique devient ainsi une membrane perméable à travers laquelle les facteurs externes viennent influencer le bâtiment qui les assimile et en diffuse le reflet médiatique. Les nouvelles technologies informatiques en temps réel permettent de générer des images en permanente variation et d'excellente qualité.

Contrairement au média visuel classique qu'est le film, la mise en scène réactive n'est plus limitée dans le temps par un début et par une fin, mais elle se recrée à chaque seconde. La qualité de la mise en scène réactive se définit par la sélection des facteurs d'influence ainsi que par une chorégraphie appropriée des images générées sur une période prolongée. La mise en scène réactive convient ainsi parfaitement à la mise en scène de base des façades médiatiques.

Los parámetros externos generan una infinita variedad de imágenes

Los medios digitales permiten que la escenificación de una fachada mediática haga referencia directa a los sucesos de la ciudad y del medio. El observador puede ser captado allí donde se encuentre en ese preciso momento –por ejemplo bajo la lluvia–. Con cámaras, sensores y modernas tecnologías de softwares se pueden capturar los parámetros externos en tiempo real y hacer uso de ellos en la escenificación. En ese caso, las fachadas mediáticas reaccionan a las alteraciones del medio como conducidas por una mano fantasmal. Factores influyentes mesurables son por ejemplo el tiempo, las condiciones de luz y el nivel de ruido del entorno, así como datos cuantitativos tales como el curso de la Bolsa o la densidad del tráfico vial del lugar. La fachada mediática se convierte así en una membrana permeable que plasma en la piel del edificio los factores externos condicionantes. Nuevas tecnologías a tiempo real provenientes del sector de los juegos informáticos hacen posible generar imágenes en variación continua y presentarlas con alta calidad.

A diferencia del medio visual clásico del film, la escenificación reactiva ya no está limitada temporalmente por un principio o un final, sino que se regenera segundo a segundo. La calidad de la puesta en escena reactiva se define por la elección de los factores influyentes y por una adecuada coreografía de las imágenes producidas durante un dilatado espacio temporal. Ello hace que la escenificación reactiva resulte óptima como programación de base de las fachadas mediáticas.

Parametri esterni che creano infinite variazioni d'immagine

I media digitali consentono, con la messa in scena di una facciata mediatica, di fare riferimenti immediati agli eventi in corso nella città e nell'ambiente. L'osservatore può essere ripreso nel punto in cui si trova, ad esempio sotto la pioggia. Attraverso l'uso di videocamere a sensori di movimento e tecnologie software all'avanguardia, i parametri esterni possono essere registrati in tempo reale e utilizzati per la messa in scena. La facciata mediatica reagisce quindi, come guidata da uno spirito, alle variazioni dell'ambiente circostante. Fattori d'influenza misurabili sono ad esempio il tempo atmosferico, le variazioni di luce o i rumori di fondo, ma anche dati quantitativi, come ad esempio le quotazioni di borsa o le condizioni del traffico. La facciata mediatica diviene così una membrana permeabile, attraverso la quale fattori d'influenza esterni agiscono sulla superficie dell'edificio, vengono da essa recepiti e restituiti come mezzo di comunicazione. Le nuove tecnologie "in tempo reale" prese a prestito dal settore dei videogiochi consentono di generare immagini con variazioni costanti e di rappresentarle in alta definizione.

Diversamente dal filmato, un mezzo di comunicazione visiva classico, la messa in scena reattiva non è più limitata nel tempo da un inizio e una fine, ma si rinnova ogni secondo. La qualità della messa in scena reattiva viene definita dalla scelta dei fattori d'influenza e da una adeguata coreografia delle immagini generate in un arco di tempo piuttosto lungo. In questo senso, la messa in scena reattiva è particolarmente adatta a formare uno sfondo in costante movimento per la facciata mediatica.

LANDMARK
CONGRESS CENTRE | ZURICH
Concept: 2004
Architect: Helmut Jahn

As part of a design competition for a congress centre for the ETH-Zurich, Helmut Jahn designed a concept situated on a prominent place at the river Limat in the centre of Zurich. The building has the form of a large spinnaker. On Helmut Jahn's request ag4 planned a panel structure furnished with LEDs – a transparent media facade which also functions as sunscreen for the "spinnaker".

The media content for the media facade is analogue to the building's shape, i.e. a large, medialised spinnaker. Sensors measure the actual winds, and modern software converts the data to generate a virtual sail in real time that blows in the wind. The programming plays on the familiar cultural ritual of showing one's colours. Analogue to using real sails the virtual sail on the media facade is set and pulled in. The building acts as a landmark not only for the city of Zurich but also for the region, and therefore the programming can also be understood along the lines: "He who shouts loudest has something to say!" The media facade has turned into an interface of the city. It captures current events and mirrors these on a 40,000 square metre area. The virtual spinnaker serves as a moveable stage for information on events inside the congress centre, the city's flag as well as emotional and atmospheric animations.

Helmut Jahn entwickelte für einen geladenen Ideenwettbewerb der ETH-Zürich einen Entwurf für ein Kongress-gebäude, das sich an prominenter Stelle am Fluss Limat im Zentrum Zürichs befinden sollte. Das Gebäude hat die Gestalt eines großen Spinnakersegels. Als vorgelagerter Sonnenschutz des "Spinnakersegels" hat ag4 auf Bitte von Helmut Jahn eine mit LEDs bestückte Lamellenstruktur geplant - eine Transparente Medienfassade.

Die Bespielung der Medienfassade ist analog der Gestalt des Gebäudes ein großes, mediales Spinnaker. Die realen Windkräfte werden mit Sensoren gemessen. Modernste Softwaretechnologie nutzt die Daten, um aus ihnen in Echtzeit ein virtuelles Segel zu generieren und dieses wie ein reales Segel in den Wind zu stellen. Die Medialisierung spielt mit dem vertrauten, kulturellen Ritual des Flaggezeigens. Analog zum Einsatz realer Segel werden die Inhalte der Medienfassade durch Einholen bzw. Setzen des virtuellen Segels ausgetauscht. Als Landmark ragt das Gebäude weit über die Stadt hinaus und so gilt für die Bespielung das Motto: "Wer den Kopf aus der Menge reckt, der hat auch was zu sagen!" Die Medienfassade wird zum Interface der Stadt, das die aktuellen Geschehnisse in der Stadt erfasst und auf einer Fläche von 40.000 Quadratmetern medial spiegelt. Als Basisbespielung wird das virtuelle Segel zur bewegten Bühne von Inhalten wie Informationen zu Veranstaltungen im Kongressgebäude, der Stadtflagge sowie emotionalen und atmosphärischen Animationen.

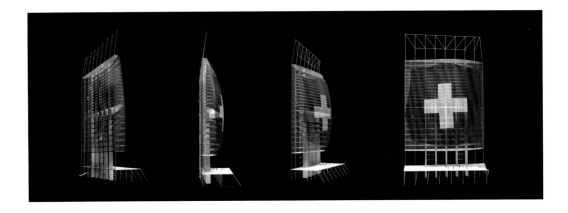

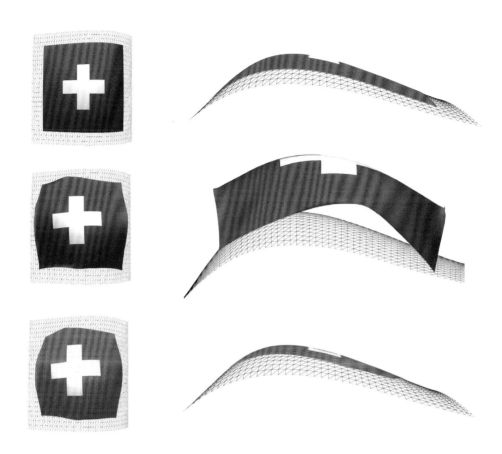

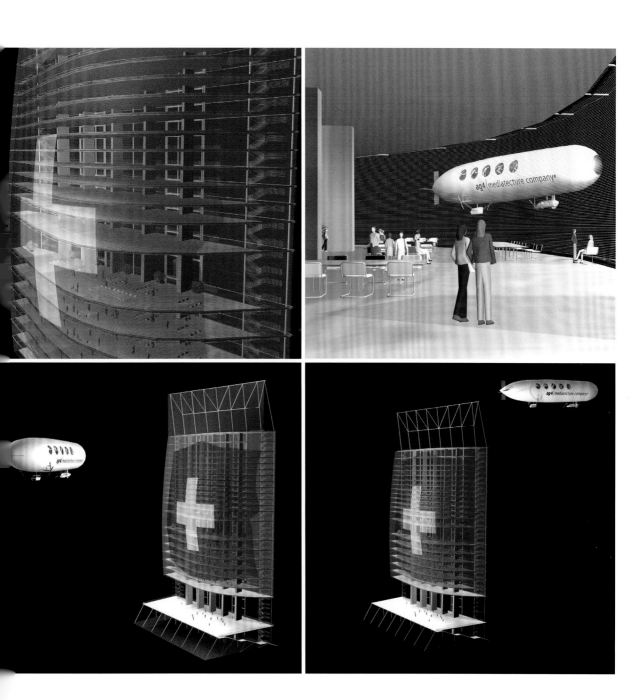

Dans le cadre d'un concours d'idées sur invitation organisé par l'ETH de Zurich, Helmut Jahn a créé un projet de palais des congrès prévu à un emplacement de marque, le long du fleuve Limat, au centre de Zurich. Le bâtiment ressemble à une grande voile de spinnaker. Pour protéger la « voile de spinnaker » du soleil, Helmut Jahn a chargé ag4 d'élaborer une façade médiatique transparente à base de lamelles équipées de DEL.

Comme le bâtiment, la mise en scène de la façade médiatique fait penser à un grand spinnaker. Des capteurs mesurent l'énergie éolienne et une technologie de logiciel ultra-moderne exploite les données enregistrées pour générer en temps réel une voile virtuelle et l'exposer au vent. La mise en scène médiatique joue sur le rituel familier et culturel du drapeau qui « annonce la couleur ». Comme pour les voiles réelles, la voile virtuelle est tour à tour rentrée ou sortie, permettant aux différentes images de se succéder sur la façade médiatique. Le bâtiment, qui représente un véritable point de repère, dépasse largement la ville ; la mise en scène médiatique s'articule autour du thème : « celui qui sort la tête de la foule a obligatoirement quelque-chose à dire ! » La façade médiatique devient l'interface de la ville, enregistrant les évènements qui s'y déroulent et les retransmettant sur une surface de 40 000 mètres carrés. La diffusion de base, la voile virtuelle, se transforme en scène animée composée d'informations relatives aux manifestations organisées par le Palais des Congrès, du drapeau de la ville, d'animations émotionnelles et d'ambiance.

Helmut Jahn concibió para un concurso de ideas convocado por la Escuela Técnica Superior Confederada de Zúrich el proyecto de un edificio del Congreso que iba a estar situado en una zona señalada del centro de Zúrich a orillas del río Limmat. La construcción tiene la forma de una gran vela de spinnaker. Como sistema de protección contra el sol instalado delante de la "vela del spinnaker", ag4 ha planeado a petición de Helmut Jahn una estructura de láminas provistas de LEDs: una fachada mediática transparente.

En analogía con la forma del edificio, la escenificación de la fachada mediática representa un gran spinnaker. La fuerza real de los vientos es medida por sensores. La tecnología de los softwares más modernos emplea esos datos para generar a tiempo real una vela virtual y ponerla a merced de los vientos como si se tratase de una vela real. La

mediatización juega con el popular ritual cultural de mostrar la bandera. Imitando el empleo habitual de una vela en la realidad, los contenidos de la fachada mediática se intercambian arriando o izando la vela virtual. En su calidad de lugar emblemático, el edificio destaca por su altura en la ciudad; por ello, a la escenificación se le puede aplicar el siguiente lema: "La cabeza que destaca por encima de la muchedumbre tiene algo que decir". La fachada mediática se convierte así en interfaz de la ciudad: recopila los sucesos urbanos de actualidad y los proyecta en una superficie de 40.000 metros cuadrados. En la escenificación de base, la vela virtual hace de plataforma dinámica de contenidos tales como informaciones sobre los actos que se celebran en el edificio del Congreso, de la bandera de la ciudad y de imágenes atmosféricas y emocionales.

In occasione di un concorso di idee indetto dal Politecnico Federale (ETH) di Zurigo, Helmut Jahn ha presentato un progetto per il Palazzo dei Congressi da costruirsi in un'area centrale di pregio, lungo il fiume Limat. L'edificio doveva avere l'aspetto formale di un grande "spinnaker". Su richiesta di Helmut Jahn e con funzione di frangisole, è stata realizzata da ag4 una struttura a lamelle dotata di LED luminosi – una facciata mediatica trasparente.

La messa in scena della facciata mediatica riprende l'aspetto dell'edificio, ossia si presenta come un grande spinnaker mediatico. La reale forza del vento viene misurata da appositi sensori. Una tecnologia software all'avanguardia utilizza i dati per generare una vela virtuale e farla gonfiare dal vento come una vera vela. La medializzazione gioca con il ben collaudato rituale culturale delle segnalazioni con bandiere. Proprio come accade realmente nell'impiego di una vela, i contenuti della facciata mediatica si avvicendano ammainando o issando la vela virtuale. In quanto punto di riferimento, l'edificio svetta da lontano sul piano della città e anche per la messa in scena vale il motto: "Chi alza la testa per emergere dalla folla ha qualcosa da dire!". La facciata mediatica ha inoltre la funzione di interfaccia con la città, registrando gli eventi in corso e resituendoli amplificati su una superficie di 40.000 metri quadrati. Come messa in scena di base, la vela virtuale si fa scenario in movimento di contenuti diversi, come informazioni sugli eventi in corso al Palazzo dei Congressi, lo stendardo con i colori della città e animazioni riferite al tempo atmosferico o alle emozioni.

URBAN
INTERNATIONAL MEDIA AVENUE | BEIJING
Concept: 2003
Architect: Albert Speer

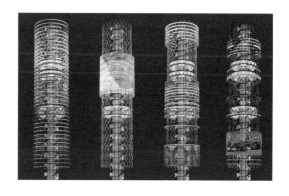

Beijing held a design-competition in order to explore possible visions of the new urban development of a three kilometre long avenue with offices for media companies. ag4 in cooperation with Albert Speer's architectural practice developed a concept for the medialisation of the central square of this Media Avenue.

The square is circular and surrounded by high-rise buildings. The concept is designed around a "media ring" of transparent media facades that are installed on the individual facades. Synchronisation of the content enables the medial crossing of space between the high-rise blocks – the "media ring" turns into a large scale panorama. The programme specially designed for this ring is an animation consisting of lots of coloured horizontal areas in combination with video clips to provide a complex choreography of the place.

The centre of the square, itself 300 metres in diameter, is occupied by a 100 metre tall tower that acts as a landmark. It consists of computer controlled moveable medialised rings. This makes not only the medialisation of the whole length of the tower possible but also enables smaller medialisations by concentrating individual rings resulting in ring monitors with a high enough resolution to broadcast live events. Both the control of the panels and the display of the media facade react to outside influences such as traffic and light. The manifold possibilities that are afforded by the display content and ring arrangement result in the tower reinventing itself continuously anew.

Im Rahmen eines geladenen Ideenwettbewerbs suchte die Stadt Peking nach Visionen für die städtebauliche Gestaltung einer drei Kilometer langen Avenue, an der sich Medienfirmen ansiedeln sollten. In Zusammenarbeit mit dem Architekturbüro Albert Speer entwickelte ag4 das Konzept für die mediale Bespielung des zentralen Platzes dieser Media Avenue.

Der Platz ist kreisförmig von Hochhäusern umschlossen und das Konzept sieht einen „Medienring" aus Transparenten Medienfassaden vor, die an den einzelnen Hochhäusern montiert sind. Eine Synchronisierung der Bespielungen macht es möglich, den Raum zwischen den Hochhäusern medial zu überbrücken – der „Medienring" wird zu einem großen Panorama. Für diesen Ring wurde ein Bespielung entwickelt, die eine Animation mit vielen horizontal bewegten Farbflächen in Kombination mit Videoclips zu einer komplexen Choreographie des Ortes werden lässt.

In der Mitte des Platzes mit einem Durchmesser von 300 Metern steht als weithin sichtbares Zeichen ein 100 Meter hoher Turm. Der Turm besteht aus medialisierten Ringen, deren Position computergesteuert verändert werden kann. Damit kann er einerseits in seiner gesamten Höhe bespielt werden, andererseits sind durch eine Konzentration der medialen Ringe kleinere Bespielungszonen möglich. Es entstehen Ringmonitore mit einer Auflösung, die auch für Live-Übertragungen genutzt werden kann. Sowohl die Steuerung der Ringe als auch die Bespielung der Medienfassaden reagiert auf äußere Einflüsse wie den Autoverkehr und das Licht. Durch die vielfältigen Kombinationsmöglichkeiten zwischen Bespielung und Ringeinteilung erfindet sich der Turm ständig neu.

Dans le cadre d'un concours, la ville de Pékin était à la recherche d'idées visionnaires pour l'aménagement urbanistique d'une avenue de 3 km, le long de laquelle plusieurs entreprises audiovisuelles envisageaient de s'implanter. En coopération avec le bureau d'architectes Albert Speer, ag4 a élaboré le concept de mise en scène médiatique de la place centrale de cette « Media Avenue ».

La place circulaire est entourée de tour et le concept prévoit un « anneau médiatique » composé de façades médiatiques transparentes installées sur les différents tour. Une synchronisation des mises en scène médiatiques permet de surmonter l'espace entre les édifices – transformant « l'anneau médiatique » en panorama géant. La mise en scène médiatique imaginée pour cet anneau transforme une animation composée de nombreuses surfaces colorées se déplaçant horizontalement et combinées à des clips vidéo en une chorégraphie complexe du lieu.

Au milieu de la place de 300 mètres de diamètre se dresse une tour de 100 m de hauteur et visible de très loin. Ses anneaux forment le support de la mise en scène médiatique ; leur position peut être modifiée par ordinateur. Ainsi, il est possible de diffuser une animation sur toute la hauteur de la tour, ou au contraire de concentrer les anneaux à un endroit précis afin de réduire la surface de la mise en scène médiatique. La haute résolution des moniteurs en forme d'anneaux permet également des retransmissions en direct. Le déplacement des anneaux et l'animation des façades médiatiques réagissent aux influences extérieures telles que le trafic automobile ou la lumière. Grâce aux innombrables combinaisons possibles entre diffusion et position des anneaux, la tour revêt sans cesse un nouvel aspect.

La ciudad de Pekín convocó un concurso de ideas en busca de visiones para la concepción urbanística de una avenida de tres kilómetros de longitud en la que tendrían sus sedes empresas relacionadas con los medios de comunicación. En colaboración con el despacho de arquitectos de Albert Speer, ag4 desarrolló el concepto para la escenificación mediática de la plaza central de esta Media Avenue.

La plaza está rodeada en círculo por rascacielos y el concepto prevé un "anillo mediático" de fachadas transparentes mediáticas, instaladas respectivamente en cada uno de los edificios. Una sincronización de las escenificaciones hace posible tender puentes virtuales entre los distintos rascacielos: el "anillo mediático" a modo de gran panorámica. Para este anillo se concibió un programa mediático que convierte en una compleja coreografía del lugar una puesta en escena de numerosas superficies dinámicas de colores horizontales combinadas con vídeo clips.

La plaza, que tiene un diámetro de 300 metros, alberga en su centro un elemento visible a gran distancia: una torre de 100 metros de altura. La torre consta de anillos mediáticos, cuya posición puede ser alterada por medio de un ordenador. Ello permite la puesta en escena de la torre en toda su longitud o bien, concentrando los anillos, que la escenificación se limite a zonas más pequeñas. Resultan así monitores circulares con una resolución que puede ser incluso utilizada para trasmisiones en directo. Tanto el control de los anillos como la escenificación de las fachadas mediáticas reaccionan ante influencias externas, por ejemplo la circulación vial o la luz. Gracias a la gran variedad de posibilidades de combinación entre la escenificación y la distribución de los anillos, la torre ofrece un aspecto siempre diferente.

Nell'ambito di un concorso di idee a invito, la città di Pechino era alla ricerca di proposte per l'organizzazione urbanistica di un viale lungo tre chilometri sul quale avrebbero trovato sede gli uffici di varie aziende del settore della comunicazione. In collaborazione con lo studio di architettura Albert Speer, ag4 ha firmato il progetto per la messa in scena mediatica del piazzale al centro di questa Media Avenue.

Il piazzale è racchiuso tra alti palazzi e il progetto prevede un "anello mediatico" costituito da facciate mediatiche trasparenti installate sui singoli grattacieli. La sincronizzazione delle messe in scena rende possibile superare virtualmente lo spazio tra i grattacieli, di modo che l' "anello mediatico" diventa una vasta ripresa panoramica. A questo scopo è stata ideata una messa in scena particolare che viene trasformata in complessa coreografia del luogo da un'animazione con tante fasce di colore orizzontali in movimento, in abbinamento con videoclip.

Al centro del piazzale, che ha un diametro di 300 metri, si trova una torre alta 100 metri, visibile da lontano come simbolo del luogo. Questa è costituita da anelli medializzati la cui posizione può essere modificata via computer. Da un lato la torre può essere medializzata a tutta altezza, mentre dall'altro, grazie alla concentrazione degli anelli è stato possibile creare aree per la messa in scena più piccole. Ne risultano monitor circolari con risoluzione adatta anche per la trasmissione di eventi dal vivo. Sia il moto degli anelli che la messa in scena delle facciate reagiscono agli influssi esterni, come le condizioni di luce e il traffico urbano. Grazie alla variegata gamma di possibilità di combinazione tra messa in scena e raggruppamento degli anelli, la torre cambia continuamente aspetto.

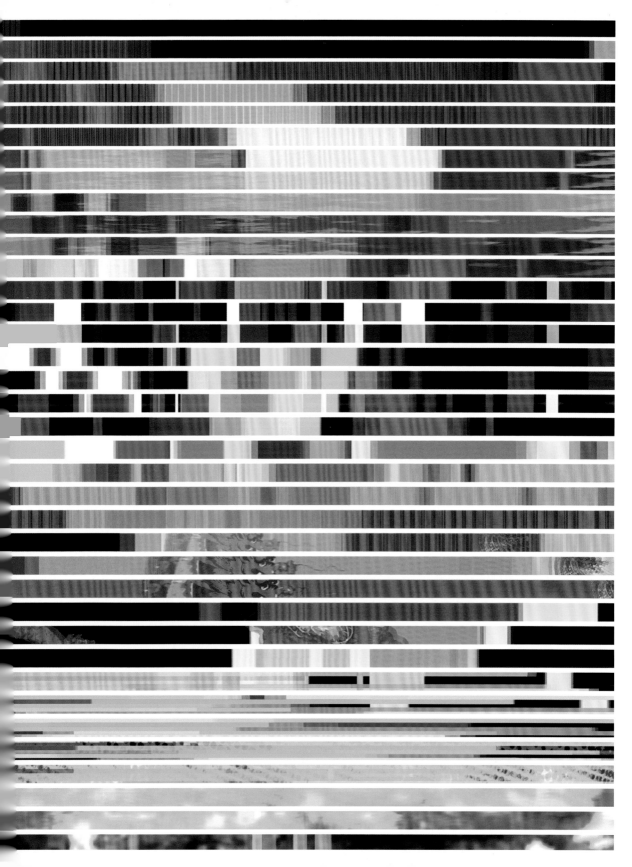

GRID
CCTV BROADCASTING STATION | BEIJING
Concept: 2004
Architects: Office for Metropolitan
Architecture (OMA, Rem Koolhaas)

In 2002 the OMA was awarded the contract for building the Chinese state television broadcasting station CCTV in Beijing. The plan to medialise the facade was part of the original submission. The challenge lay in finding an economically viable way of medialising of the complex and 230 metre tall building that was economically viable. ag4 managed to develop just such a concept.

The building's structure is mirrored by a large scale, circular diagonal latticing on the facade. A first approach would furnish only this structure with LEDs. However, limiting the LEDs to the latticing drastically reduces the area covered by media facade. Despite the low resolution necessitated by the latticing there is a surprising spectrum of moving images that can be displayed. A second approach consists of the medialisation of the facade's vertical profiles. This would create a larger medialised area and therefore a more succinct depiction. However, it is also more cost intensive.

The LED structure of the media facade enables the depiction of animated fonts and images over the whole length of the building. The reactive media programming consisting of changing colours and forms and reacts to external influences such as traffic, light and wind.

Das OMA gewann 2002 den Wettbewerb für einen Neubau des chinesischen Staatsfernsehens CCTV in Peking. Von Anfang an war eine Medialisierung der Fassade geplant. Die Herausforderung dabei lag in der Frage, wo und wie die komplexe und 230 Meter hohe Gebäudeskulptur mit einer finanzierbaren Lösung medialisiert werden kann. ag4 entwickelte ein Konzept, das dieses Problem lösen kann.

Die statische Konstruktion des Gebäudes zeichnet sich auf seiner Fassade in einer großflächigen, diagonal umlaufenden Gitterstruktur ab. Ein erster Lösungsansatz sieht vor, LEDs nur in diese diagonale Struktur zu integrieren. Die Reduktion der LEDs auf das konstruktive Gitter führt dabei zu einer extremen Flächenreduktion der Medienfassade. Trotz der sehr groben Struktur bietet sich bei bewegten Bildern ein erstaunliches Spektrum an Darstellungsmöglichkeiten. Ein zweiter Lösungsansatz besteht in der alleinigen Bespielung der vertikalen Fassadenprofile. Dieser Ansatz schafft eine größere medialisierte Fläche und damit eine prägnantere Darstellung, ist aber dementsprechend kostenintensiver.

Die LED-Struktur der Medienfassade erlaubt die Darstellung von animierter Schrift und Bildgrafiken in kompletter Gebäudehöhe. Eine reaktive Basisbespielung mit Farb- und Formbewegungen reagiert auf externe Parameter der Umgebung wie Verkehr, Licht und Wind.

L'OMA a remporté en 2002 le premier prix du concours organisé pour la nouvelle construction du bâtiment de la télévision chinoise d'Etat CCTV à Pékin. La mise en scène médiatique de la façade était prévue depuis le début. Le défi consistait à trouver un moyen finançable de mettre en scène la sculpture du bâtiment d'une hauteur de 230 m. Ce problème a pu être réglé grâce au concept développé par ag4.

La construction statique du bâtiment se caractérise par une vaste structure grillagée diagonale entourant le bâtiment. Une première solution consiste à intégrer des DEL à cette structure diagonale. La réduction des diodes à la grille de la construction entraîne une réduction importante de la surface de la façade médiatique. Malgré la structure très grossière, il est possible de diffuser une quantité impressionnante d'animations différentes sur la façade médiatique. Une seconde solution consiste à mettre en scène uniquement les profils verticaux de la façade. Cette solution permet de médialiser une surface plus importante et d'obtenir ainsi une mise en scène plus marquante. Mais elle est aussi plus coûteuse.

La structure DEL de la façade médiatique permet la diffusion de textes animés et d'images graphiques sur toute la hauteur du bâtiment. Une mise en scène réactive de base composée de mouvements de différentes couleurs et de différentes formes réagit à des paramètres de l'environnement extérieur comme le trafic, la lumière ou encore le vent.

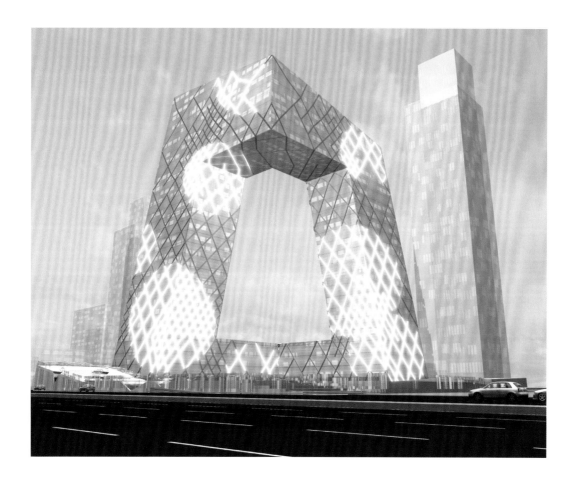

La OMA ganó el concurso convocado en 2002 para la construcción de un edificio de nueva planta para la sede de la Televisión Central China (CCTV) en Pekín. Desde el principio se planeó una fachada mediática. El desafío lo planteaba en este caso la cuestión de dónde y cómo llevar a cabo la mediatización de este complejo edificio-escultura de 230 metros de altura con una solución financiable. ag4 concibió un concepto que puede resolver el problema.

La construcción estática del edificio se manifiesta en su fachada con una estructura reticular en diagonal que cubre una gran superficie. Una primera solución prevé integrar LEDs sólo en esa estructura diagonal. La limitación de los LEDs a la retícula supone una reducción drástica de superficie de fachada mediática. Pese a que la estructura es muy ruda, resulta asombroso el espectro de posibilidades de presentación de imágenes en movimiento que ofrece. Una segunda solución opta por introducir la escenificación exclusivamente en los perfiles verticales de la fachada. Esta última solución genera una mayor superficie mediatizada y, de ese modo, una presentación más precisa, pero sus costes son en consecuencia también mayores.

La estructura de LEDs de la fachada mediática permite mostrar texto e imágenes gráficas en movimiento en toda la altura del edificio. Una escenificación de base reactiva de formas y colores móviles reacciona a parámetros externos del entorno como el tráfico, la luz y el viento.

Lo studio OMA ha vinto nel 2002 il concorso per la nuova costruzione a Pechino della sede della CCTV, la televisione pubblica cinese. La medializzazione della facciata è stata programmata sin dall'inizio. La sfida era in questo caso nello studio di come e in che punto si potesse medializzare una struttura articolata e complessa come quella dell'edificio, alto 230 metri, con una soluzione sostenibile dal punto di vista economico. Il progetto di ag4 prevede la soluzione di questo problema.

La costruzione statica dell'edificio è caratterizzata dalla facciata costituita da un reticolato a linee diagonali. Una prima impostazione del progetto prevede l'integrazione dei LED solo in questa struttura diagonale. La riduzione dei LED sul reticolato porta a sua volta a una cospicua riduzione della superficie della facciata mediatica. A dispetto

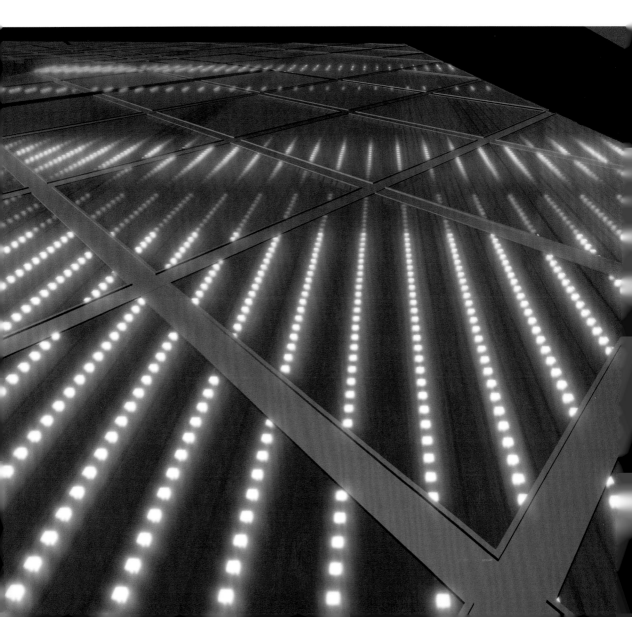

della vastità della struttura, con le immagini in movimento si ottiene una sorprendente varietà di possibili rappresentazioni. Una seconda proposta consiste nella medializzazione solo dei profili della facciata. In questo modo si ottiene una superficie medializzata più grande e quindi la possibilità di rappresentare immagini più pregnanti, ma la soluzione è anche relativamente più costosa.

La struttura a LED della facciata mediatica consente la rappresentazione di scritte e immagini grafiche su tutta l'altezza dell'edificio. La messa in scena di base reattiva, con forme e colori in movimento, reagisce ai parametri esterni di provenienza ambientale, come la luce, le condizioni del traffico e la presenza di vento.

THE PEARL
MEDIA ENVIRONMENT | DUBAI
Concept: 2004

ag4 mediatecture company® was approached to design a medialisation concept for the future district „Dubai Pearl" in Dubai. The neighbourhood consists of single high-rise blocks arranged in a circle. However, the middle of the circle is not occupied by a public urban space but is a roofed and air-conditioned interior space. The task therefore consisted of making the medialisation accessible from a great variety of perspectives.

At the centre of the design is a light weight spherical construction in the form of an orb which is suspended between the individual high-rise blocks. The orb has a diameter of 50 metres and its bionic construction guarantees maximal stability at an extremely low weight. The construction is furnished with LEDs and can thus be entirely medialised. The orb turns into a shining pearl while the high-rise blocks become mother-of-pearl shells for the medialised pearl. The ensemble consisting of high-rise blocks and the pearl is now a widely visible and intelligible sign – Dubai Pearl. The interior of the orb can be utilized as a lounge or an exhibition area.

The reactive content of the medialisation covers the orb with flowing colours that react on environmental influences. It is, of course, possible, to change the media programme to include advertisements.

ag4 mediatecture company® wurde angefragt, für das zukünftige Stadtviertel „Dubai Pearl" in Dubai eine Medialisierung zu entwerfen. Das Stadtviertel besteht aus einzelnen, ringförmig angeordneten Hochhäusern. In der Mitte des Rings befindet sich jedoch kein urbaner Außenraum, sondern ein weiterer überbauter und klimatisierter Innenraum. Aufgabe war es, die Medialisierung aus vielen Perspektiven erlebbar zu machen.

Im Zentrum des Entwurfs steht ein Leichtbaukörper in Kugelform, der zwischen die Hochhäuser gespannt ist. Der Körper hat einen Durchmesser von 50 Metern und seine bionische Konstruktion gewährleistet maximale Stabilität bei geringster Gewichtlast. Die Konstruktion ist mit LEDs bestückt und kann so vollständig medialisiert werden. Die Kugel wird zur glitzernd schillernden Perle, die Hochhäuser werden zur perlmuttartig reflektierenden Schale der medialisierten Perle. Das Ensemble aus Hochhäusern und Perle wird zu einem weithin sichtbaren und verständlichen Zeichen – Dubai Pearl. Der Innenraum der Kugel kann erschlossen und zum Beispiel als Lounge oder Ausstellungsraum genutzt werden.

Die reaktive Bespielung verzaubert die Kugel mit einem fließenden Farbspiel, das auf die äußeren Umwelteinflüsse reagiert. Die Implementierung von Werbung in die Bespielung ist möglich.

ag4 mediatecture company® a été priée d'élaborer d'un concept de mise en scène médiatique pour le futur quartier « Dubai Pearl » de Dubaï. Le quartier est composé de tours isolées, disposées en cercle. Au milieu du cercle, cependant, il n'y a pas d'espace extérieur urbain, mais un espace intérieur climatisé équipé d'une superstructure. La mission consistait à imaginer une mise en scène médiatique pouvant être perçue sous plusieurs perspectives.

Le projet s'articule autour d'un élément de construction légère en forme de globe tendu entre les différents immeubles. La construction bionique de cet élément de 50 mètres de diamètre garantit une stabilité maximale pour une charge de poids la plus réduite possible. La construction est équipée de DEL qui permettent une mise en scène totale. Le globe se transforme en perle scintillante et chatoyante et les tours en coquilles aux reflets nacrés. L'ensemble qu'ils composent devient alors un symbole visible et compréhensible par tous – Dubai Pearl. L'espace intérieur du globe peut être viabilisé et aménagé par exemple en salon ou en salle d'exposition.

La diffusion réactive anime le globe d'un jeu de couleurs qui réagissent aux influences de l'environnement. Il est possible d'intégrer des messages publicitaires à la diffusion.

ag4 mediatecture company® recibió el encargo de proyectar un concepto mediático para el futuro distrito urbano de Dubai "Dubai Pearl". El distrito se compone de rascacielos no adosados dispuestos formando un círculo. En el centro del círculo, sin embargo, no existe una zona urbana al aire libre sino otro espacio interior sobreedificado y climatizado. La tarea consistía en hacer que la mediatización fuera perceptible desde diversas perspectivas.

El punto central del proyecto es un cuerpo luminoso con forma de esfera tensado entre los edificios. Este cuerpo tiene un diámetro de 50 metros y su construcción bioelectrónica garantiza la máxima estabilidad con el menor suplemento de peso. La esfera está equipada con LEDs, lo que permite la mediatización de toda su superficie. La esfera se convierte en una brillante perla resplandeciente; los rascacielos devienen piel reflectante nacarada de la perla mediática. El conjunto formado por los edificios y la perla se transforma así en un símbolo visible a gran distancia y de fácil interpretación: Dubai Pearl. El interior de la esfera puede cerrarse y utilizarse, por ejemplo, como sala de reunión o de exposición.

La escenificación reactiva hechiza la bola con un fluido juego colorista que reacciona ante las influencias externas del entorno. También es posible introducir publicidad en la escenificación.

ag4 mediatecture company® ha ricevuto l'incarico di sviluppare un progetto per la medializzazione del futuro quartiere "Dubai Pearl" nella capitale degli Emirati Arabi Uniti, costituito da singoli grattacieli disposti in cerchio. Al centro dell'anello non vi è tuttavia uno spazio urbano esterno ben definito, ma uno spazio costruito, chiuso e climatizzato. Scopo del progetto era rendere la medializzazione fruibile da più prospettive diverse.

Nucleo centrale del progetto è un corpo sferico in materiale da costruzione leggero posizionato tra i grattacieli, con un diametro di 50 metri e di stabilità garantita, grazie a una costruzione avveniristica in cui i carichi sono ridotti al minimo. La costruzione è corredata di LED luminosi e può pertanto essere completamente medializzata. La sfera si trasforma in perla dalla luce opalescente, mentre i palazzi tutto attorno diventano il guscio riflettente, la madreperla virtuale della perla medializzata. L'insieme grattacieli–perla diviene così un segno caratteristico, visibile da lontano e di comprensione immediata: Dubai Pearl. Lo spazio interno alla sfera può essere aperto e utilizzato, ad esempio, come salone per ricevimenti o esposizioni e mostre.

La messa in scena reattiva conferisce alla sfera un'atmosfera magica con giochi di colore che si susseguono in modo fluido, in grado di reagire agli influssi dell'ambiente esterno. Nella messa in scena è possibile inoltre anche l'implementazione di comunicati pubblicitari.

BLOB
MULTIFUNCTION ARENA | BEIJING
Concept: 2003
Architect: Thomas Glöckner

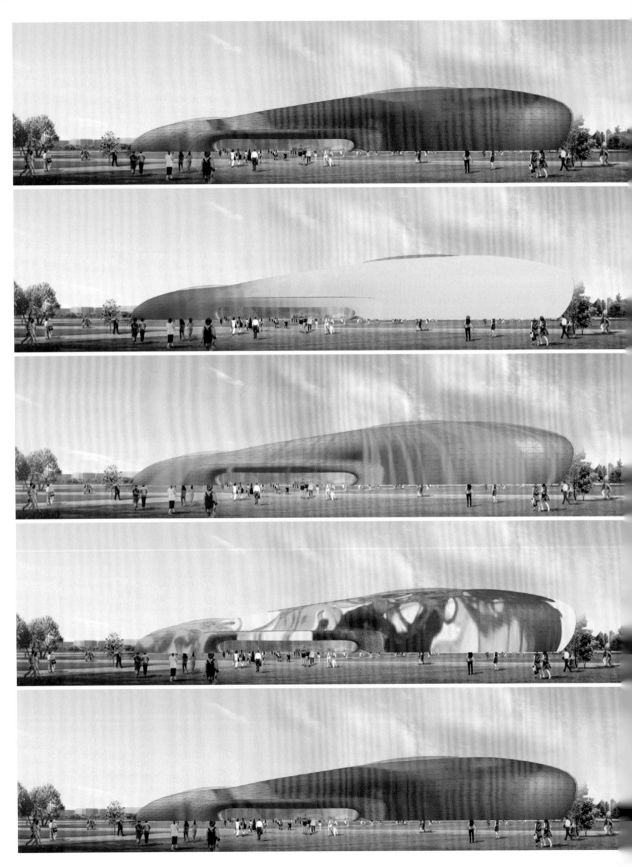

In 2002 the architect Thomas Glöckner won the competition for the new multifunction arena in Beijing which is part of the Olympic Games 2008 project. His design is based on the form of an eight lying on its axis – a Chinese sign for luck.

The architectural outer skin of the arena consists of a semi-transparent plastic which enables the communication of dynamic light designs from the inside to the outside. Pipes with LEDs are placed into the space between the building's outer layer and the insulation. Despite the low resolution caused by the small amount of LEDs, the outer layer's opacity compensates for this, thus affording great effects very economically.

The media content is based – analogue to the building's shape – on organic aesthetics generated reactively to environmental influences. At all times the media content has two centres which are positioned in the two eyes of the lying eight – an effect which underlines the formal concept and makes it more apparent from the point of view of the passer-by. Areas with a higher resolution are capable of displaying video images and entertainment.

2002 gewann der Architekt Thomas Glöckner den Wettbewerb für die neue Multifunktionshalle in Peking anlässlich der Olympischen Spiele 2008. Sein Entwurf basiert auf der Form einer liegenden Acht, die in der chinesischen Kultur ein Zeichen für Glück repräsentiert.

Die architektonische Außenhaut der Halle besteht aus einem halbtransparenten Kunststoff und kann damit auch ein dynamisches Lichtdesign von Innen aufnehmen und wiedergeben. In den Konstruktionsraum zwischen Außenhaut und Dämmung sind Rohre mit Leuchtdioden eingesetzt. Trotz einer geringen Auflösung durch wenige LED-Bildpunkte ist durch die diffuse Außenhaut eine hohe und dennoch kostengünstige inszenatorische Wirkung erreichbar.

Die Bespielung basiert – analog der Form des Gebäudes – auf einer organischen Ästhetik, die reaktiv von den äußeren Umwelteinflüssen generiert wird. Die Bespielung hat stets zwei Zentren, die sich in den beiden Augen der liegenden Acht befinden und so das formale Konzept der Architektur auch aus Fußgängerperspektive erleb- und sichtbar machen. An Stellen mit einer höheren Bildauflösung können Videobilder mit Information und Entertainment geschaltet werden.

En 2002, l'architecte Thomas Glöckner a remporté le premier prix du concours organisé pour la nouvelle salle polyvalente de Pékin réalisée dans le cadre des Jeux Olympiques de 2008. Son projet repose sur la forme d'un huit allongé, qui représente dans la culture chinoise un symbole de bonheur.

La peau est en matière est en matière synthétique translucide pouvant recevoir un éclairage dynamique de l'intérieur et le renvoyer vers l'extérieur. Des tuyaux équipés de DEL ont été installés dans l'espace situé entre le revêtement extérieur et l'isolation. La résolution est basse en raison du nombre réduit de points d'images DEL, mais le revêtement extérieur diffus permet malgré tout d'obtenir une mise en scène réussie à frais réduits.

La mise en scène est basée sur une esthétique organique rappelant la forme du bâtiment et générée de manière réactive par les influences de l'environnement. Les deux centres de diffusion se trouvent au milieu des deux boucles du huit, rendant le concept architectural également visible et discernable d'une perspective piétonnière. Les surfaces à haute résolution peuvent être utilisées pour diffuser des images vidéo informatives ou divertissantes.

En 2002, el arquitecto Thomas Glöckner ganó el concurso para la construcción de un nuevo pabellón multifuncional en Pekín con motivo de los Juegos Olímpicos de 2008. Su proyecto tiene una planta en forma de ocho, que en la cultura china es un número asociado con la buena suerte.

La piel arquitectónica externa del pabellón es de material plástico semitransparente y puede por tanto captar un diseño dinámico de luces del interior y reproducirlo. En el espacio constructivo existente entre la piel exterior y el aislamiento, hay instalados tubos con diodos luminiscentes. Pese a la escasa resolución por el bajo número de píxels, la calidad difusa de la piel exterior permite conseguir un gran efecto escenográfico con costes favorables.

La escenificación se basa –análogamente a la forma del edificio– en una estética orgánica que es generada de forma reactiva por las influencias medioambientales externas. La puesta en escena tiene siempre dos centros, que se encuentran en ambos ojos del ocho de la planta, haciendo de ese modo visible y perceptible el concepto formal de la arquitectura también desde la perspectiva del transeúnte. En las zonas con mayor resolución pueden emitirse imágenes de vídeo informativas o de carácter lúdico.

Nel 2002 l'architetto Thomas Glöckner è risultato vincitore del concorso per un nuovo spazio multifunzionale a Pechino, in occasione dei Giochi Olimpici del 2008. Il progetto è basato sulla forma di un "otto" disteso, che nella cultura cinese è simbolo di buona fortuna.

Il "guscio" architettonico esterno di questo spazio è in materiale plastico traslucido e si presta quindi molto bene a ricevere e a riprodurre all'esterno la disposizione dinamica delle luci interne. Nello spazio costruttivo tra guscio esterno e sistema d'isolamento sono inseriti tubi contenenti i LED luminosi. La risoluzione non è alta, in quanto il numero di punti LED è ridotto, ma con l'effetto luminoso diffuso attraverso il guscio esterno si ottiene comunque, e senza eccedere nei costi, un ottimo effetto scenografico.

La messa in scena è basata - seguendo la forma dell'edificio - su un tipo di estetica organico, che viene generato in modo reattivo direttamente dagli influssi ambientali esterni. Essa presenta sempre due punti centrali, disposti nei due cerchi dell' "otto" disteso, rendendo quindi la concezione formale dell'architetura visibile e fruibile anche dalla prospettiva di chi passa a piedi. Nelle zone con risoluzione maggiore è possibile trasmettere immagini video, informazioni e intrattenimento.

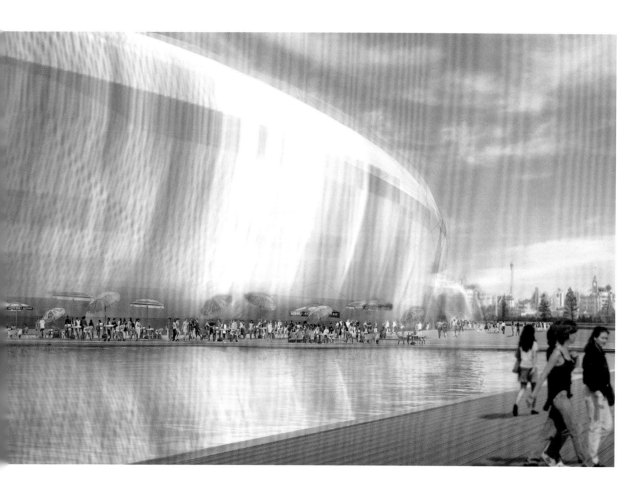

Audi planned to have a showroom designed by Helmut Jahn on the orbital ring in Munich. Using a specially staged presence, Audi wanted to use a transparent media facade to set itself apart from neighbouring competition. The challenge in designing the media facade lay in making it noticeable for the traffic streaming past. This was achieved by arranging the vertical panels of the transparent media facade in such a way that their axis faces the oncoming traffic.

A graphic, self-generating media content reacts in real time to the traffic. Horizontal bars in the Audi colours white and grey visualise the current traffic situation. The way the medialised bars interact in a playful manner with and against the traffic has the media facade interact with the traffic.

ag4 used the special magic of the transparent media facade in order to merge the media content with the showroom behind. Special areas which are not medialised stay black and grant an unhindered view into the showroom with the effect of literally framing the cars and making them the centre of attention. Especially at night vehicles can be staged medially through a light design that is coordinated together with the media content of the media facade. One side of the transparent media facade has the panels set back a few metres into the showroom itself – the virtual world interlocks with its real counterpart and becomes a dominating stylistic element.

This project did not come to fruition because Munich town planning guidelines do not allow moving electronic images in the public domain. Munich's rejection of the media facade was one of the main reasons for Audi's decision not to settle in Munich.

Audi plante in einem Gebäude von Helmut Jahn am Mittleren Ring in München einen Showroom einzurichten. Durch eine besonders inszenierte Präsenz vor Ort wollte Audi sich mit einer Transparenten Medienfassade positiv von der Konkurrenz in der Nachbarschaft abgrenzen. Die Herausforderung bei der Gestaltung der Medienfassade lag darin, auch vom vorbeiströmenden Verkehr gut wahrgenommen zu werden. Dies wurde erreicht, indem die vertikalen Lamellen der Transparenten Medienfassade sich in ihrer Achse dem entgegenkommenden Verkehr zuwenden.

Eine grafische, sich selbst generierende Basisbespielung reagiert in Echtzeit auf den vorbeifließenden Autoverkehr. Horizontale Balken in den Audi-Markenfarben Weiß und Grau visualisieren die jeweilige Verkehrssituation. Indem die medialisierten Balken sich spielerisch mit und gegen den Verkehr bewegen, treten die Medienfassade und der Autoverkehr in Interaktion.

ag4 setzte die besondere Magie der Transparenten Medienfassade ein, um die mediale Bespielung mit dem dahinterliegenden Showroom zu verschmelzen. Nicht bespielte Schwarzanteile machen den Showroom an gezielten Stellen komplett einsehbar. Wie in einem Bilderrahmen werden die Autos so gezielt herausgestellt. Besonders nachts können die Fahrzeuge mit einem Lichtdesign, das mit der Bespielung der Medienfassade synchronisiert ist, medial inszeniert werden. An einer Seite der Transparenten Medienfassade sind die Lamellen um einige Meter in den Ausstellungsraum versetzt - die virtuelle Welt verzahnt sich mit der realen und wird zu einem raumprägenden Gestaltungselement.

Das Projekt konnte nicht realisiert werden, da die städtebaulichen Vorgaben der Stadt München keine bewegten, elektronischen Bilder im öffentlichen Raum erlauben. Die Ablehnung der Medienfassade durch die Stadt München war ein wesentlicher Grund dafür, dass Audi auf den Standort München verzichtete.

Audi
Audi
Audi

Audi envisageait d'aménager un showroom dans un bâtiment de Helmut Jahn sur le Mittlerer Ring de Munich. Grâce à une façade médiatique transparente lui permettant de se mettre en scène de façon particulière, Audi espérait se démarquer positivement de la concurrence voisine. Le défi de cette façade médiatique consistait à attirer également l'attention du trafic automobile. Le problème fut réglé en tournant les lamelles verticales de la façade médiatique transparente sur leur propre axe, vers le trafic routier arrivant en face.

Une mise en scène graphique de base auto-générée réagit en temps réel au trafic automobile. Des barres horizontales aux couleurs de la marque Audi – blanc et gris – retransmettent l'état de la situation routière. Les barres servant de support à la mise en scène se déplacent en jouant avec le trafic routier, allant à sa rencontre ou se mouvant avec lui, et la façade médiatique interagit ainsi avec le trafic automobile.

ag4 a exploité la magie particulière d'une façade médiatique transparente pour faire fusionner la mise en scène médiatique et le showroom placé derrière. Des parties de la façade non incluses à la diffusion rendent le showroom entièrement visible à certains endroits. De nuit, en particulier, les véhicules peuvent faire l'objet d'une mise en scène basée sur un éclairage synchronisé avec les images diffusées par la façade médiatique.

Sur une partie de la façade médiatique transparente, les lamelles sont déplacées de quelques mètres dans la salle d'exposition – le monde virtuel fusionne avec le monde réel et se transforme en élément conceptuel caractéristique de l'espace.

Le projet n'a pas pu être réalisé car le cahier des charges urbanistiques de la ville de Munich ne permet pas la diffusion d'images électroniques animées dans les espaces publics. Ce refus de la façade médiatique par la ville de Munich fut l'un des motifs essentiels qui ont poussé Audi à s'installer ailleurs.

Audi tenía previsto instalar una sala de exposición en un edificio de Helmut Hahn situado en el Mittlerer Ring, una vía de circunvalación de Múnich. La idea perseguida por Audi era desmarcarse de la competencia establecida en el vecindario con una fachada mediática transparente que resaltase con originalidad su presencia en el lugar. El desafío a la hora de diseñar la fachada mediática consistía en conseguir llamar la atención también del numeroso tráfico que por allí circula. Ello se logró orientando al tráfico que llega de cara los ejes de las láminas verticales de la fachada mediática transparente.

Una escenificación gráfica de base de generación propia reacciona a tiempo real al tráfico automovilístico que circula por delante. Recuadros con los colores blanco y gris de la marca visualizan la situación vial del momento. Moviendo juguetonamente los recuadros virtuales con y en contra de la circulación, la fachada mediática y el tráfico vial entran en interacción.

ag4 empleó la magia especial de la fachada mediática transparente para fundir lo que en ella se muestra con la sala de exposición que se abre tras ella. Zonas en negro sin mediatización consiguen hacer completamente reconocibles áreas específicas de la sala de exposición. De ese modo, determinados automóviles se exhiben como rodeados por el marco de un cuadro. Sobre todo por la noche, permite una presentación mediática de los automóviles con un diseño de luces que está sincronizado con la escenificación de la fachada. En un lado de la fachada mediática transparente, las láminas penetran varios metros en la sala de exposición: el mundo virtual se funde con el real y se transforma en un elemento decorativo de gran efecto espacial.

El proyecto no pudo realizarse debido a que la normativa urbanística de la ciudad de Múnich no permite ningún tipo de imágenes electrónicas en movimiento en el exterior. El rechazo de la fachada mediática por la ciudad fue un factor decisivo para que Audi renunciara a este emplazamiento en Múnich.

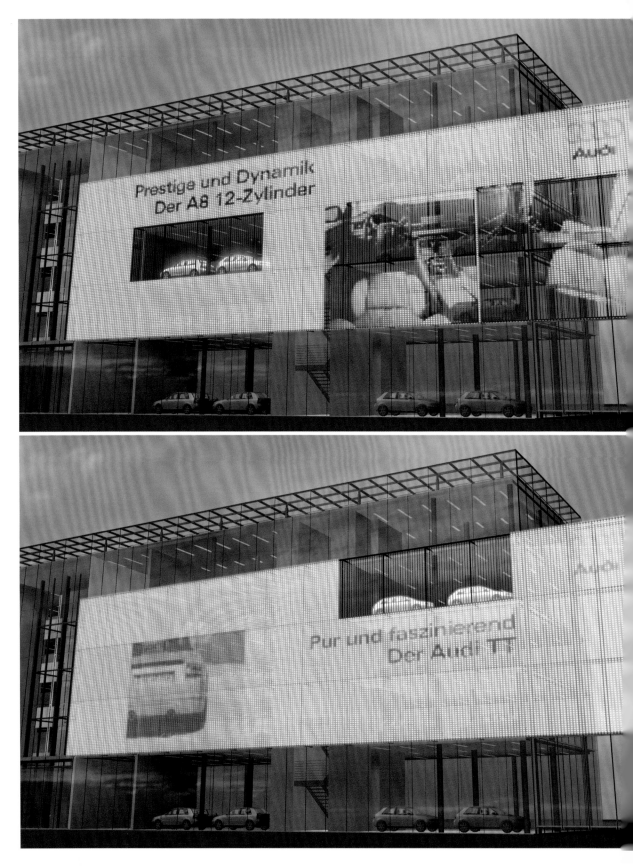

La Audi intendeva realizzare uno showroom all'interno di un edificio a firma di Helmut Jahn, sulla circonvallazione Mittlerer Ring di Monaco di Baviera. Proprio attraverso una presenza particolarmente scenografica sul posto prescelto, il desiderio dell'azienda era di distinguersi positivamente, con una facciata mediatica trasparente, dalla concorrenza con sede nei dintorni. Nella creazione della facciata il problema da risolvere era come catturare lo sguardo anche degli automobilisti in transito sulla circonvallazione. Per ottenere questo risultato, le lamelle verticali della facciata mediatica sono orientate in direzione del traffico in arrivo.

Una messa in scena grafica e autogenerata reagisce in tempo reale alle condizioni di traffico momento per momento. Barre orizzontali nei colori di bandiera della Audi, grigio e bianco, visualizzano la situazione del traffico presente. Poiché le barre medializzate si muovono in modo ludico con il traffico stesso e in direzione di esso, facciata mediatica e traffico entrano in interazione reciproca.

ag4 ha utilizzato la magia tutta particolare della facciata mediatica trasparente per fondere la messa in scena mediatica con la presenza dello showroom retrostante. Alcune aree "spente" rendono completamente invisibile determinate zone dello showroom. Come in una cornice, alcune auto vengono perciò escluse dalla rappresentazione. Particolarmente nelle ore serali e notturne diventa possibile proiettare in modo medializzato sulla facciata i veicoli con un gioco di luci sincronizzato con la messa in scena della facciata stessa. Su un lato della facciata le lamelle sono spostate di qualche metro nel salone - di modo che il mondo virtuale si aggancia con quello reale e diviene un elemento creativo di forte impatto.

Non è stato possibile realizzare il progetto perché le norme urbanistiche della città di Monaco non consentono la rappresentazione di immagini elettroniche in movimento in spazi pubblici. La bocciatura del progetto di facciata mediatica da parte del comune di Monaco è stata la ragione essenziale della rinuncia da parte dell'Audi alla realizzazione dello showroom nella capitale della Baviera.

TIME
RAILWAY TOWER IN THE SONY CENTER | BERLIN
Concept: 2000
Architect: Helmut Jahn

In the year 2000 the Deutsche Bahn AG moved into the high-rise block at the Sony Center Potsdamer Platz in Berlin. ag4 developed a medialisation concept for the facade which should display the presence of Deutsche Bahn for all to see.

The construction of the facade, however, would not allow for a belated installation of panels on the outside. Instead, existing sunscreen panels on the inside of the high-rise block are replaced by panels with inlaid LEDs. Similar to the sunscreen panels, the new installation is adjustable.

It was only the invention of the railway and the subsequent introduction of timetables that required time to be standardised. The classical railway station clock has thus become an integral part of public life. At the same time it became a distinctive icon for the railway. Its medialisation on the facade of the company's headquarters thus turns it to a modern icon of the 21st century.

Die Deutsche Bahn AG hat im Jahr 2000 das Hochhaus am Sony Center Potsdamer Platz in Berlin bezogen. ag4 entwickelte ein Medialisierungskonzept für die Fassade, das die Präsenz der Deutschen Bahn weithin sichtbar zeigen sollte.

Die Konstruktion der Fassade des Hochhauses lässt eine nachträglich installierte, außenliegende Montage der Lamellen nicht mehr zu. Stattdessen werden die vorhandenen innenliegenden Sonnenschutzlamellen durch Lamellen ausgetauscht, die mit LEDs bestückt sind. Diese Lamellen sind wie herkömmliche Sonnenschutzlamellen weiter justierbar.

Erst die Erfindung der Eisenbahn mit ihrem zeitbezogenen Fahrplan hat eine exakte, an allen Orten gleiche und für alle lesbare Uhrzeit notwendig gemacht. Die klassische Bahnhofsuhr ist so zu einem integralen Bestandteil des öffentlichen Lebens und zum markanten Zeichen der Bahn geworden. Ihre Medialisierung auf der Fassade der Firmenzentrale der Bahn macht sie zu einem modernen Zeichen des 21. Jahrhunderts.

La société allemande des chemins de fer « Deutsche Bahn AG » a emménagé en l'an 2000 dans le building du Sony Center de Berlin, situé sur la Potsdamer Platz. ag4 a imaginé le concept de mise en scène médiatique de la façade, dont l'objectif était d'attirer de loin l'attention du public sur la présence de la « Deutsche Bahn ».

La construction de la façade ne permet pas l'installation a posteriori de lamelles sur la structure extérieure. A la place, les jalousies ont été remplacées par des lamelles équipées de DEL. Ces nouvelles lamelles sont ajustables, comme les lamelles traditionnelles.

C'est de l'invention des chemins de fer avec ses horaires fixes qu'est née la nécessité de créer une heure universelle et lisible par tous. Ainsi, l'horloge de la gare fait dorénavant partie intégrante de la vie publique ; elle est même devenue l'emblème de la société des chemins de fer. Sa mise en scène médiatique sur la façade de la centrale de l'entreprise la transforme en symbole moderne du XXIe siècle.

La empresa de ferrocarriles alemana Deutsche Bahn AG ocupó el año 2000 el rascacielos de oficinas del Sony Center en la Potsdamer Platz de Berlín. ag4 desarrolló un concepto mediático para la fachada que tenía como objetivo destacar a gran distancia la presencia de la Deutsche Bahn.

El tipo de construcción de la fachada de este rascacielos no permite que se instale en el exterior una estructura añadida de láminas. En su lugar, las láminas de las persianas colocadas en el interior para regular la luz solar se sustituyen por otras equipadas con LEDs. Estas láminas siguen siendo regulables como las de las persianas.

La invención del ferrocarril con sus horarios ha hecho necesaria la hora exacta, coincidente en todos los lugares y legible para cualquiera. El clásico reloj de estación es en este sentido una parte integral de la vida pública y se ha convertido en un rasgo característico del ferrocarril. Su adaptación mediática en la fachada de la central de la empresa de ferrocarriles hace de él un símbolo moderno de siglo XXI.

La sede berlinese delle ferrovie tedesche, Deutsche Bahn AG, dal 2000 si trova nel grattacielo del Sony Center, nella Potsdamer Platz. ag4 ha realizzato il progetto di medializzazione della facciata, con lo scopo di rendere visibile da lontano la presenza della Deutsche Bahn come azienda.

La modalità di costruzione della facciata non permette il montaggio in un secondo tempo delle lamelle dall'esterno. Al posto di una struttura lamellare applicata esternamente, le tende frangisole tipo veneziana già esistenti all'interno sono state sostituite con lamelle dotate di LED luminosi, regolabili a piacere esattamente come normali tende alla veneziana.

Con l'invenzione delle ferrovie e la diffusione degli orari dei treni, gli orologi, regolati tutti alla stessa ora e leggibili da tutti, sono divenuti un elemento irrinunciabile. Il classico orologio da stazione ferroviaria è diventato così parte integrante della vita pubblica e caratteristica importante del luogo. La medializzazione sulla facciata delle sede centrale delle Ferrovie lo rende un moderno simbolo del 21° secolo.

ag4 | mediatecture company®

ag4 mediatecture company® was established in 1991 as a result of the cooperation between architects and media designers. ag4 is short for the German for "consortium for four-dimensional construction". The first years of cooperation saw the rise of a new creative discipline which ag4 established in 1993 and termed "mediatecture".

ag4 mediatecture company® works primarily for large institutions and companies with a vital need for communication – both internally and externally. ag4 assists its clients with mediatectural methods in the establishing and communication of their corporate identity. The focus of ag4 consists of achieving interaction between the virtual world of the corporation and the actual piece of architecture by the integration of media into the building itself. This objective means ag4 is active in three business streams: media facades, space presentation and electronic systems resulting in communication solutions that are developed and realised by ag4 as a full service provider.

Architect Christoph Kronhagel and business economist Ralf Müller are managing partners of ag4 while the director Harald Singer is a dormant partner. Together they lead a team consisting of many professions. The multidisciplinarity as well as the high degree of identification with the company of the long-serving team members form the basis of the success of the projects. Artistic ambitions and economic thinking work hand in hand resulting in innovative solutions that are artistically inspired.

www.ag4.de

1991 entstand ag4 mediatecture company® als Zusammenschluss von Architekten und Mediendesignern. ag4 steht für „Arbeitsgemeinschaft für vierdimensionales Bauen". Die ersten Jahre der Zusammenarbeit in dieser Arbeitsgemeinschaft brachten eine neue gestalterische Disziplin hervor, die ag4 1993 mit dem Begriff der „Mediatektur" etablierte.

ag4 mediatecture company® arbeitet vornehmlich für große Institutionen und Unternehmen, die ein vitales Kommunikationsbedürfnis nach Innen und Außen haben. ag4 unterstützt ihre Kunden mit mediatektonischen Maßnahmen bei Aufbau und Kommunikation ihrer Unternehmensidentität. Im Fokus des Schaffens steht, durch die Integration von Medien in die Architektur die virtuellen Welten des Unternehmens mit den konkreten Orten der Architektur zu verbinden. Mit dieser Zielsetzung ist ag4 in drei Geschäftsbereichen tätig: Medienfassaden, Rauminszenierungen und Elektronische Systeme. Es entstehen Kommunikationslösungen, die von ag4 als Full-Service-Dienstleister entwickelt und umgesetzt werden.

Architekt Christoph Kronhagel und Betriebswirt Ralf Müller sind die handelnden Gesellschafter der ag4, der Regisseur Harald Singer ist stiller Gesellschafter. Sie leiten ein Team, das sich aus vielfältigen Professionen zusammensetzt. Die Interdisziplinarität sowie die hohe Identifikation der langjährigen Teammitglieder mit der Idee und Arbeitsweise von ag4 sind Grundlage für den Erfolg der Projekte. Künstlerische Ambitionen und wirtschaftliches Handeln fließen dabei eng ineinander. Es entstehen innovative Lösungen, die künstlerisch inspiriert sind.

www.ag4.de

ag4 mediatecture company® a été créée en 1991 et réunit des architectes et des spécialistes du design médiatique. Le sigle ag4 signifie « Arbeitsgemeinschaft für vierdimensionales Bauen » (Groupe de travail pour les constructions quadridimensionnelles). Au cours des premières années, ce groupe de travail a engendré une nouvelle discipline créatrice qui fut établie en 1993 par ag4 sous le nom de « médiatecture ».

ag4 mediatecture company® travaille principalement pour de grandes institutions et entreprises pour lesquelles la communication interne et externe représente un besoin vital. ag4 assiste ses clients en leur soumettant des mesures médiatiques et architectoniques qui leur permettent de développer et de communiquer l'identité de leur entreprise. Le principe créateur consiste, en intégrant les médias à l'architecture, à établir le lien entre les mondes virtuels de l'entreprise et les sites concrets d'architecture. ag4 poursuit cet objectif dans trois secteurs d'activité : les façades médiatiques, les mises en scène dans l'espace et les systèmes électroniques. Les solutions de communication proposées par ag4 sont réalisées de leur développement à leur mise en ?uvre par le prestataire global.

L'architecte Christoph Kronhagel et le gestionnaire d'entreprise Ralf Müller sont les associés gérants d'ag4, le metteur en scène Harald Singer étant associé occulte. Ils dirigent une équipe regroupant les professions les plus diverses. Le caractère interdisciplinaire de l'équipe et la forte identification de ses membres de longue date à l'idée et aux méthodes de travail de ag4 sont à l'origine du succès des projets réalisés. Les ambitions artistiques et l'activité économique sont étroitement liées. Les solutions innovatrices qui voient le jour sont le fruit d'une inspiration artistique.

www.ag4.de

ag4 mediatecture company® se fundó en 1991 como agrupación de arquitectos y diseñadores mediáticos. ag4 es la abreviatura de la correspondencia alemana de "colectivo para la construcción tetradimensional". Los primeros años de colaboración de este colectivo trajeron consigo el surgimiento de una nueva disciplina creativa que ag4 designó en 1993 con el término "mediatectura".

ag4 mediatecture company® trabaja primordialmente para grandes empresas e instituciones que tienen necesidad vital de comunicación tanto hacia el exterior como interna. Con medidas mediatectónicas, ag4 contribuye a edificar y a trasmitir la identidad empresarial de sus clientes. Su objetivo central es conectar los mundos virtuales de la empresa con los lugares concretos de la arquitectura mediante la integración de los medios de comunicación en la arquitectura. ag4 trabaja con esa meta en tres sectores económicos: fachadas mediáticas, escenificaciones espaciales y sistemas electrónicos. Soluciones comunicativas que ag4 desarrolla e instala, ofreciendo una prestación completa de servicios.

El arquitecto Christoph Kronhagel y el empresario Ralf Müller son los socios activos de ag4, el director Harald Singer es un socio capitalista. El equipo que dirigen integra profesiones diversas. La interdisciplinariedad y la gran identificación de los miembros de esta agrupación de muchos años con la idea y el modo operativo de ag4 son la base del éxito de este proyecto, que interconecta las ambiciones creativas y la actividad económica. Soluciones innovadoras inspiradas artísticamente.

www.ag4.de

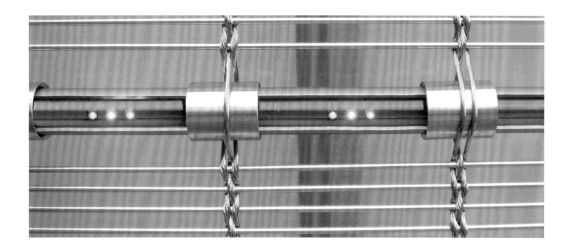

ag4 mediatecture company® nasce nel 1991 come associazione di architetti e media designer. ag4 è un acronimo per "Arbeitsgemeinschaft für vierdimensionales Bauen", ossia "Gruppo di lavoro per costruzioni in quattro dimensioni". I primi anni di collaborazione hanno portato alla nascita di una nuova disciplina creativa, che nel 1993 ag4 ha definito con il concetto di "mediatecture".

ag4 mediatecture company® lavora soprattutto per grandi aziende e istituzioni per le quali l'esigenza di comunicare tra l'interno e l'esterno è essenziale. ag4 assiste i propri clienti con soluzioni "mediatettoniche" nella costruzione e comunicazione della loro identità aziendale. Al centro di tutto c'è l'unione del mondo virtuale dell'azienda con i luoghi concreti dell'architettura, attraverso l'integrazione dei media nell'architettura stessa. Con questo scopo, ag4 si muove in tre campi d'attività: facciate mediatiche, installazioni ambientali e sistemi elettronici. Ne derivano soluzioni comunicative che vengono sviluppate e messe in pratica da ag4, un centro di servizi "full service".

Christoph Kronhagel, architetto, e Ralf Müller, laureato in economia, sono i soci commerciali di ag4, mentre il registra Harald Singer è socio occulto. Sono alla guida di un gruppo che si compone di tante professionalità diverse. L'interdisciplinarietà e la profonda identificazione da parte dei membri del gruppo con l'idea di fondo e le modalità di lavoro di ag4 sono alla base di tanti progetti di successo. Ambizioni artistiche e gestione economica si intrecciano in piena armonia, dando vita a soluzioni innovative, ma sempre ispirate all'arte.

www.ag4.de

The Media Facade as Part of Urban Culture by Christoph Kronhagel

The need to electronically medialise buildings is a growing phenomenon all over the world – and not without reason. Lets have a look at how electronic medialisation influences the urban environment: a totally rigid structure such as a facade suddenly starts moving. This movement is not in any way related the building's functionality, it is totally free and independent – it is magic. The outer layer of the building is enchanted, something new may occur any second. The media facade provides us with the chance to emotionalise our environment. Perhaps this is linked to the indeterminate longing that our built-up environment should not only be functional-rational but that it is capable of becoming a place that touches us much more deeply – namely in our soul and complex our moods. The recent architectural development mirrors a growing need for higher complexity. Perhaps we require living spaces that correspond more closely to our inner tensions and moods. Are we therefore looking for a correlation between our inner life and the outside world? The human soul is ridden by diremption: on the one hand we require clear boundaries that govern our lives while on the other hand we start rebelling against them as soon as they are deemed not to correspond to our perceived inner life. Therefore, anything that remains open, anything that is not exactly defined bears an innate attraction. That is why we love anything that is veiled in magic. Every time we get to know a secret we hope that our own life is not sealed off within itself, that there is more out there.

Vision

The contemporary situation of our built-up environment, however, makes the possibility to display just such magic feasible. Not only that, but the economic pressures to do so are considerable. Our cities are mostly made up of a relatively random sequence of buildings whose interplay hardly gives the impression of secrecy. This is where the media facade comes in: it is capable of breaking up the constructive insularity of facades and manages to relate them dynamically to each other in an urban context. One only needs to design the media programmes of the various facades to interact with each other. Our urban environment thus gains the dimension of a sensually perceived correlation. That is why I propose for cities which already have a number of media facades to create and apply a concept for media programmes. This enables the gradual building up of a culture of holistic urban programming while at the same time preventing misuse of medialised surfaces (for example through aggressive advertising).

Change of Paradigms

A precondition for such a concept is the intensive examination of cognitive phenomena. The new medium of the media facade transforms the previously static nature of architecture into a mirror of the current existential orientation of its environment. That which is depicted and played on a media facade documents the interests of either the operator or the user to enhance the architecture of the building and the need to portray oneself to the outside world. The nature of the programme can take many directions ranging from a dynamic colourful display right through to video content. For the latter there is widespread misconception that a video programme automatically leads to uncontrolled flood of images. This fear is based on our everyday experiences with electronic media. The potential of presenting electronic images on a large surface leads those involved to apply the mechanisms of a monitor to a whole facade. Our visual habits are largely conditioned by television and we therefore expect a monitor to entertain or inform us with continuously changing and constantly new content. However, a monitor presupposes that it takes the visual centre stage. The viewer is singled out and drawn in entirely by it. This process results in the perception that a media facade should display editorial content similar to that of a television station. It is this relationship between the monitor and the viewer, however, which simply cannot exist with a medialised facade: the viewer of just such a front is all but singled out. As soon as he or she is in public space, 100% cognition of the electronic images becomes impossible because the viewer has to react to many outside influences. Even a standard advertisement with a narrative structure and a length of 30 seconds fails to impact properly in public spaces simply because it usually relies on some kind of punchline. An audience that is in motion itself cannot possibly pay the necessary attention to follow such content. As a result a programme for a media facade sets totally new standards – a great opportunity for contemporary urban culture. Interaction between the building's owners, its users, the city and current societal developments means that the parameters governing content develop continuously with the result that they have to be redefined for each new media facade project. The medialisation of our urban environment is thus elevated to a methodology of integrated reflection – it demonstrates the way we interact communally. Any programme on a media facade that causes consternation or concern of whatever kind may be changed at the drop of a hat – contrary to the architecture behind it. In a way this kind of medialisation provokes a reflection on our social competencies and interaction. It keeps on challenging the viewer to confront him/herself and to ask the questions: How do we want to be? What kind of urban atmosphere is suitable? The creative scope of the media design may yet throw many principles overboard – we should be prepared to be surprised.

Medial Urban Culture

The basis of this concept can consist of different factors of creative media design such as the rhythm and frequency with which images change, a predefined colour scale or contextual aspects. Alternatively, the focus can be shifted to the dramaturgy of coming into town so that programmes in the city centre differ to those on the main traffic arteries. Such examples – certainly not typical for architecture in general – go some way to show that the range of subjects to be considered is considerable. The development of a medial concept may well prove to be an economic factor for the entire city if not the whole even region – this is especially true in a global context. Which town can afford not to have individual marketing these days? In order for the economic circulation of capital and investors to take notice, a city has to stand. A urban media programme could stress certain aspects that serve to communicate a city's economic image. Investments into the dynamics of electronic media are very efficient, especially in the long term. A city such as Cologne, for example, can control the dramaturgic medialisation of its bridges and thus underline its claim to be of of Germany's capitals of the media and the arts. At the same time it could incorporate regional culture in the cityscape by portraying the cheerful soul so typical of the people of the Rhineland. Alone the usage of electronically medialised façades is very attractive: it proves participation in a global game in that one is modern and innovative. Or to put it differently: the medium is the message. Naturally, the content of these facades has to take into account the communicative interests of the building's users or investors. The form the media design is to take can still conform to a citywide concept. This is, of course, also an important parameter when it comes to general urban planning situations.

Outlook

The chances of success for a medialised architecture – a mediatecture – in the context of our urban environment depend largely on ourselves. They depend on what the concerned parties make of it – a complex social process. Mediatecture creates links between people and their built-up environment. The yearning for something we can call home, for regional culture is ever increasing in this global game of economic factors – a yearning mediatecture can satisfy. We "mediatects" will not only take into account the construction processes' direct requirements but also the users' communicative needs. Another factor that influences our work is the cultural situation of the location in question, the task being the direct aim of developing the site's identity. The role of the architect remains untouched by all of this. He/She will continue to provide the structure's fundamental design. The mediatect works as partner to the architect in order to expand his/her ideas and shape them to fit in with the overall framework of the media concept. This enables the development of a living space that is largely governed by the Internet and other communication media.

Die Medienfassade als Teil der Stadtkultur von Christoph Kronhagel

Überall auf der Welt wächst das Bedürfnis, Architektur elektronisch zu medialisieren – das muss Gründe haben. Schauen wir uns an, wie die elektronische Medialisierung eine gebaute Umwelt beeinflusst: Eine in sich völlig statische Konstruktion wie die einer Fassade gerät plötzlich in Bewegung. Diese Bewegung hat nichts mit der Funktionalität der Konstruktion zu tun, sie ist völlig frei und unbegrenzt – sie ist magisch. Ein Zauber legt sich über die Gebäudehaut und jeden Moment kann etwas Neues entstehen. Die Medienfassade bietet die Chance, unsere Lebensräume zu emotionalisieren. Vielleicht wird damit auch die unbestimmte Sehnsucht verbunden, dass unsere gebaute Umwelt nicht allein funktional-rationalistisch orientiert ist, sondern zu einem Ort wird, der uns wesentlich tiefer in unseren komplexen Seelenlagen zu berühren vermag. Die architektonische Entwicklung der letzten Zeit spiegelt ein wachsendes Bedürfnis nach höherer Komplexität wider. Vielleicht brauchen wir Lebensräume, die sich passender und stimmiger zu unseren inneren Spannungen und Empfindungen gesellen. Suchen wir damit vielleicht nach Authentizität zwischen unserer Innen- und Außenwelt? Es liegt eine große innere Zerrissenheit in unserem menschlichen Wesen: Einerseits brauchen wir klare Fixpunkte, an denen wir uns festhalten können, und gleichzeitig wehren wir uns auch wieder gegen diese Ordnungen, wenn sie nicht mehr authentisch mit unserer jeweils gefühlten Innenwelt sind. Deswegen ist alles, was offen bleibt und sich nicht exakt definiert, was etwas Unfassbares in sich birgt, so ungemein anziehend. Deswegen lieben wir alles, was in einer gewissen Magie erstrahlt. Jede Erfahrung eines Geheimnisses birgt die Hoffnung, dass die eigenen Lebensumstände doch nicht in sich abgeschlossen sind, dass man noch Möglichkeiten hat.

Vision

Die zeitgenössische Situation unserer gebauten Umwelt kann es sich jedoch selten leisten, eine solche Magie zu entfalten. Zu stark sind dazu die wirtschaftlichen Zwänge. Unsere Städte sind meist eine relativ zufällige Folge von Baukörpern, die es in ihrem Zusammenspiel kaum vermögen, ein Geheimnis aufzubauen. An dieser Stelle bietet die Medienfassade eine grundsätzliche Erweiterung an: Sie kann die konstruktive Abgeschlossenheit einer Fassade aufbrechen und damit im städtebaulichen Kontext Fassaden zueinander dynamisch in Beziehung setzen. Sie braucht dazu nur die Bespielungsinhalte der verschiedenen Gebäude mediengestalterisch miteinander abzugleichen. Dadurch kann der städtische Raum die Qualität eines sinnlich wahrnehmbaren Zusammenhangs wieder zurückgewinnen. Deswegen schlage ich vor, dass Städte mit mehreren Medienfassaden eine Gestaltungssatzung für deren Bespielungsinhalte ausarbeiten und anwenden. So kann eine ganzheitliche stadträumliche Bespielungskultur aufgebaut werden und auch dem Missbrauch der medialen Oberfläche (z.B. durch zu aggressive Werbung) Einhalt geboten werden.

Paradigmenwechsel

Die Voraussetzung für eine solche Gestaltungssatzung ist die intensive Auseinandersetzung mit Wahrnehmungsphänomenen. Das neue Medium Medienfassade transformiert die statische Haltung einer Architektur in einen Spiegel der momentanen Befindlichkeit ihrer sozialen Umwelt. Das, was auf einer medialen Haut gespielt wird, dokumentiert die Interessen des Betreibers oder Nutzers, die Architektur seines Gebäudes aufzuwerten und sich damit nach außen darzustellen. Die Mentalität der Bespielung kann sehr vielfältig sein. Sie reicht von der dynamischen Lichtgestaltung bis hin zur Videobespielung. Für den Fall videobespielter Medienfassaden gibt es die weit verbreitete Annahme, dass diese Medienfassaden automatisch zu unkontrollierten Bilderfluten führen können. Diese Befürchtung basiert auf unseren Erfahrungen mit elektronischen Bildmedien. Das Potenzial, auf einer großen Fläche elektronische Bilder zu präsentieren, verleitet die Beteiligten immer erst einmal dazu, die Mechanismen eines Monitors auf die Fassade zu übertragen. Unsere Sehgewohnheiten sind durch den Kontext Fernsehen maßgeblich konditioniert und so erwarten wir von einem Monitor, dass er uns ständig mit etwas Neuem unterhält oder informiert. Ein Monitor aber provoziert immer eine visuelle Fixierung. Er vereinzelt den Betrachter, der Betrachter wird völlig in den Bann des Mediums gezogen. Aus dieser Gewohnheit resultiert die Erwartung, dass eine Medienfassade ein redaktionelles Programm wie ein Fernsehsender aufnehmen soll. Dieser Zusammenhang existiert allerdings bei einer medialisierten Architektur nicht: Der Betrachter einer Medienfassade ist alles andere als vereinzelt. Sobald er sich im öffentlichen Raum befindet, lässt er eine hundertprozentige Wahrnehmung der elektronischen Bilder nicht zu, weil er auf zu viele Reize gleichzeitig reagieren muss. Schon ein normaler Werbeclip mit einer narrativen Struktur in einer Länge von circa 30 Sekunden funktioniert im öffentlichen Raum nicht mehr, da ein solcher Clip meist mit einer Pointe arbeitet. Die dazu notwendige Aufmerksamkeit bekommt er nicht von einem Publikum, das selbst in Bewegung ist. Die Bespielung einer Medienfassade setzt also völlig neue Maßstäbe, und genau darin liegt die Chance für eine

Stadtkultur, die zeitgemäß aufgestellt werden soll. Bei jedem neuen Medienfassadenprojekt müssen auch die inhaltlichen Parameter neu bestimmt werden. Sie entwickeln sich in einem stetigen Interaktionsprozess zwischen Besitzer bzw. Nutzer des Gebäudes, der Stadt und aktuellen gesellschaftlichen Entwicklungen. Die Medialisierung unserer gebauten Umwelt wird damit zur Methodik einer integrierten Reflexion, die darlegt, in welcher Form wir gemeinschaftlich agieren. Jede Bespielung einer Medienfassade, die in irgendeiner Art und Weise Unmut erzeugt, kann sofort geändert werden – im Gegensatz zur Architektur. In gewisser Weise provoziert diese Art der Medialisierung eine Reflexion unserer sozialen Kompetenzen und unserer gesellschaftlichen Interaktionen. Sie fordert uns ständig dazu heraus, über uns selber klar zu werden und uns zu fragen: Wie wollen wir sein? Welche Stadtatmosphäre passt zu uns? Die Kreativität des Mediendesigns kann viele Prinzipien der Bespielungskultur auswerfen – wir sollten uns hier von uns selber überraschen lassen.

Mediale Stadtkultur

Als Grundlage einer Gestaltungssatzung können verschiedene mediengestalterische Faktoren festgelegt werden, z.B. der Rhythmus der Bildwechsel, ein genauer Farbkanon oder inhaltliche Aspekte. Oder es entsteht eine genaue Dramaturgie, wie man von außen nach innen eine Stadt wahrnehmen will, so dass im Zentrum andere Inhalte aufgespielt werden als in den Einfahrtschneisen. Solche für den Architekturbetrieb sicherlich ungewöhnlichen Beispiele zeigen, dass man in sehr viele Richtungen denken muss. Die Entwicklung einer medialen Gestaltungssatzung wird eine wirtschaftliche Bedeutung für die jeweilige Stadt oder Region haben können – dies gilt erst recht im globalen Kontext. Welche Stadt kommt heute ohne ein individuelles Marketing aus? Um im ökonomischen Kreislauf des Kapitals und der Investoren wahrgenommen zu werden, muss sie sich abheben. Mittels einer medialisierten Stadtkultur können besondere Profile herausgearbeitet werden, die das wirtschaftliche Selbstverständnis eines (Stand)Ortes vermitteln. Die Investition in die Dynamik von elektronischen Medien ist hierbei langfristig sehr effizient. Eine Stadt wie Köln könnte beispielsweise seine Brücken dramaturgisch kontrolliert medialisieren und damit seinen Anspruch als Medien- und Kunststadt untermauern. Gleichzeitig ließe sich hiermit die rheinische Frohnatur inszenieren und so die regionale Kultur im Stadtbild verankern. Die Initiierung elektronisch medialisierter Fassaden hat allein schon ihren Reiz, weil man damit die Zugehörigkeit zu einem globalen Spiel beweist: Man ist innovativ und modern oder anders gesagt „The medium is the message." Die inhaltliche Ausrichtung solcher Fassaden muss aber natürlich auch immer die kommunikativen Interessen der Nutzer des jeweiligen Gebäudes bzw. des Investors dokumentieren. Die Art und Weise des Mediendesigns kann sich dabei trotzdem der Metaordnung einer städtischen Gestaltungssatzung unterordnen. Das geschieht bei der Gestaltung von Architektur und Städtebau auch nicht anders.

Ausblick

Die Chancen einer medialisierten Architektur – einer Mediatektur – für unsere gebauten Umwelten liegen in uns selbst. Es kommt darauf an, was alle Beteiligten daraus machen – es handelt sich um einen komplexen sozialen Prozess. Die Mediatektur schafft Verbindungen zwischen den Menschen und ihrer gebauten Umwelt. Die Sehnsucht nach Heimat und regionaler Kultur wird im globalen Spiel der wirtschaftlichen Kräfte immer deutlicher und kann durch Mediatektur aufgenommen werden. Wir „Mediatekten" werden dabei nicht nur auf die direkten Anforderungen des jeweiligen Bauprozesses reagieren. Wir werden die kommunikativen Bedürfnisse der Nutzer des Gebäudes mit der jeweiligen kulturellen Situation des Projektstandorts miteinander abstimmen und in Einklang bringen. Es geht darum, die Identität des Ortes herauszuarbeiten. Die Rolle des Architekten wird sich deswegen nicht ändern. Nach wie vor wird er die grundlegende Idee zu einem Bauwerk setzen. Der Mediatekt bietet sich als Partner des Architekten an, um dessen architektonische Ideen inhaltlich in die Gesamtabstimmung der medialen Ausrichtung zu übernehmen und weiterzuführen. So kann eine gebaute Umwelt entstehen, die einer Lebenswelt entspricht, die maßgeblich von Internet und anderen Kommunikationsmedien beeinflusst wird.

La façade médiatique comme élément de la culture urbaine par Christoph Kronhagel

Si la nécessité de mettre en scène l'architecture à l'aide de supports électroniques grandit actuellement partout dans le monde, ce n'est certainement pas sans raisons. Voyons comment une mise en scène électronique peut influencer un bâtiment : une construction en soi totalement statique se met tout à coup en mouvement. Ce mouvement n'a rien à voir avec la fonctionnalité de la construction, il est totalement libre et illimité – il est magique. La surface du bâtiment s'enveloppe d'un charme susceptible de faire naître à chaque instant quelque-chose de nouveau. La façade médiatique nous offre la possibilité de charger nos espaces vitaux d'émotions. Peut-être y associons-nous aussi la nostalgie indéfinie d'un environnement urbain qui ne soit pas uniquement fonctionnel et rationnel, mais plutôt un lieu capable d'interpeller en profondeur la complexité de nos états d'âme. L'évolution architecturale des dernières années reflète la nécessité croissante d'une plus grande complexité. Peut-être avons-nous besoin d'espaces vitaux capables de s'associer de manière plus appropriée et plus cohérente à nos tensions et sensations intérieures. Cela signifierait-t-il que nous sommes à la recherche d'une certaine authenticité entre notre monde intérieur et notre monde extérieur ? La nature humaine se caractérise par un grand déchirement intérieur : d'une part, nous avons besoin de repères fixes auxquels nous orienter, et d'autre part nous nous défendons contre cet ordre dès qu'il perd l'authenticité qui le rapproche du monde intérieur que nous ressentons. C'est pourquoi tout ce qui est incertain, pas exactement défini, tout ce qui recèle quelque-chose d'inconcevable devient si attrayant. C'est pourquoi nous aimons tout ce qui se nimbe d'une certaine magie. A chaque fois que nous faisons l'expérience d'un nouveau secret, nous espérons que nos propres conditions de vie ne soient finalement pas si définitives, que nous disposions encore de plusieurs possibilités.

Vision

Cependant, la situation contemporaine de l'environnement urbain qui nous entoure peut rarement se permettre de déployer une telle magie. Les contraintes économiques sont trop importantes. Nos villes sont généralement une succession plus ou moins fortuite de bâtiments dont l'unité n'est guère capable de receler un secret quelconque. C'est là que la façade médiatique offre un enrichissement fondamental : elle peut rompre l'herméticité d'une façade et permet un rapprochement dynamique des façades entre elles dans un contexte urbanistique. Il lui suffit pour cela de faire concorder les uns avec les autres les contenus de diffusion des différents bâtiments. Ainsi, l'espace urbain peut retrouver la qualité d'un contexte perceptible au niveau sensoriel. C'est pourquoi je propose que les villes disposant de plusieurs façades médiatiques élaborent et appliquent un statut conceptuel concernant leurs contenus respectifs de diffusion. Cela permettrait de développer une culture de diffusion urbaine globale et de mettre fin aux usages abusifs des surfaces médiatiques (par les publicités trop agressives par exemple).

Changement de paradigmes

Un tel statut conceptuel n'est possible qu'en procédant à une analyse intensive des phénomènes de perception. Le nouveau média que représente la façade médiatique transforme l'attitude statique d'une architecture en miroir de l'état momentané de son environnement social. Ce qui est diffusé sur le support médiatique reflète l'intérêt qu'éprouve le gérant ou l'usager à valoriser l'architecture de son bâtiment et à se présenter ainsi au monde extérieur. La mise en scène médiatique peut avoir des visages très multiples. Elle peut se présenter sous forme d'animation lumineuse dynamique ou encore de diffusion vidéo. Beaucoup supposent que les façades médiatiques à diffusion vidéo peuvent automatiquement entraîner des déluges incontrôlés d'images. Cette crainte repose sur l'expérience que nous avons des médias à base d'images électroniques. Dans un premier temps, la possibilité de présenter des images électroniques sur une vaste surface pousse toujours les intéressés à retransmettre sur la façade les mécanismes d'un écran. Nos habitudes visuelles sont fortement conditionnées par le facteur télévision : nous attendons d'un écran qu'il nous fournisse des divertissements et informations sans cesse renouvelés. Pourtant, un écran provoque toujours une fixation visuelle. Il isole l'observateur ; ce dernier se laisse totalement captiver par le média. C'est sur la base de cette habitude que nous attendons d'une façade médiatique qu'elle diffuse un programme rédactionnel - comme une chaîne de télévision. Cependant, une architecture faisant l'objet d'une mise en scène médiatique ne peut pas offrir cette connexité : l'observateur d'une façade médiatique n'est pas isolé, bien au contraire. Lorsqu'il se trouve dans un espace public, il est exclu qu'il perçoive la totalité des images électroniques dans la mesure où il doit réagir à une quantité trop importante de stimuli. Un film publicitaire normal à structure narrative et d'une longueur d'environ 30 secondes est inconcevable dans un espace public, car un spot de la sorte fonctionne normalement uniquement avec une pointe. La mise en scène d'une façade médiatique établit donc des critères totalement nouveaux, et c'est justement là l'occasion que se doit de saisir une culture urbaine soucieuse de se mettre en scène dans l'esprit du temps. A chaque nouveau projet de façade médiatique, les paramètres de contenu doivent eux aussi être redéfinis. Ils évoluent dans un processus constant d'interaction entre le propriétaire ou l'usager du bâtiment, la ville et les évolutions sociales actuelles. La mise en scène médiatique de notre environnement urbain se transforme ainsi en méthodologie d'une réflexion intégrée qui reflète la façon dont nous nous comportons en communauté. Dès que la mise en scène d'une façade médiatique provoque d'une manière ou d'une autre le mécontentement, elle peut être modifiée immédiatement – contrairement à l'architecture. D'une certaine manière, cette forme de mise en scène médiatique provoque une réflexion de nos compétences et de nos interactions sociales. Elle nous pousse sans cesse à une réflexion sur nous-mêmes et à la question : Qui voulons-nous être ? Quelle est l'atmosphère urbaine qui nous convient ? Le caractère créatif du design médiatique peut générer de nombreux principes de la culture de diffusion – à nous de nous laisser surprendre par nous-mêmes.

Culture urbaine médiatique

Différents facteurs de création médiatique peuvent être définis comme base d'un statut conceptuel : le rythme du changement d'images, un canon de couleurs particulier, ou encore plusieurs aspects liés au contenu. Ou alors on détermine une véritable dramaturgie de la manière dont la ville est censée être perçue de l'extérieur vers l'intérieur, et on programme en centre-ville des mises en scène médiatiques totalement différentes de celles des grands axes d'arrivée dans la ville. Ces exemples certainement insolites pour l'activité architecturale montrent qu'il convient de réfléchir à plusieurs niveaux. Le développement d'un statut conceptuel médiatique peut avoir une signification économique pour la ville ou la région concernée – en particulier dans un contexte global. De nos jours, quelle ville peut se passer d'un marketing individuel ? Pour avoir une chance d'être remarquée parmi la masse des capitaux et investisseurs, chaque ville doit se profiler. La mise en scène médiatique d'une culture urbaine permet de dégager des profils particuliers dont l'objectif est de transmettre l'image économique d'un site ou d'un lieu. Dans cet objectif, investir dans le dynamisme de médias électroniques se révèle très efficace à long terme. Une ville comme Cologne, par exemple, pourrait procéder à une mise en scène médiatique contrôlée de ses ponts pour souligner son caractère de ville médiatique et artistique. Cela permettrait également de mettre en scène la gaîté de caractère de cette région rhénane et d'ancrer la culture régionale dans le paysage urbain. La création de façades médiatiques électroniques est attirante, ne serait-ce que parce que celles-ci nous permettent de prouver notre appartenance à un jeu global : elles montrent que nous sommes innovateurs et modernes ; en un mot, « the medium is the message ». L'orientation du contenu de ce type de façades, cependant, doit bien entendu refléter les intérêts de l'usager du bâtiment ou de l'investisseur en matière de communication. Mais le design médiatique d'une façade peut tout de même se subordonner à l'organisation d'un statut conceptuel urbain global. L'aménagement architectural et urbanistique ne fonctionnent pas autrement.

Perspectives

Nous sommes les seuls à décider quelles sont les opportunités que peut offrir la mise en scène médiatique d'une architecture – une « médiatecture » - à notre environnement urbain. Cela dépend des personnes concernées – il s'agit d'un processus social complexe. La médiatecture établit une relation entre les hommes et leur environnement urbain. La nostalgie d'une patrie et d'une culture régionale prend de plus en plus d'importance face à la globalisation des puissances économiques ; la médiatecture est une possibilité d'y répondre. Nous, les « médiatectes », ne réagissons pas uniquement aux exigences directes des différents processus d'urbanisme. Nous concilions et harmonisons les besoins des usagers du bâtiment en matière de communication avec la situation culturelle du site faisant l'objet du projet. Il s'agit de mettre en valeur l'identité du lieu. Le rôle de l'architecte ne changera pas pour autant. Il restera le responsable de l'idée fondamentale à l'origine d'un bâtiment. Le médiatecte se considère comme un partenaire potentiel de l'architecte, lui offrant de reprendre ses idées architecturales et d'y rester fidèle dans l'élaboration d'un concept global de mise en scène médiatique. Cela permet la naissance d'un environnement urbain en adéquation avec un univers fortement influencé par Internet et autres moyens de communication.

La fachada mediática como parte de la cultura urbana Christoph Kronhagel

En todo el mundo se reclama cada vez más la mediatización electrónica de la arquitectura. Alguna razón debe de haber para ello. Veamos cómo obra en el entorno edificado una mediatización de estas características - una construcción completamente estática, como es una fachada, de repente se pone en movimiento. Este movimiento no tiene nada que ver con la funcionalidad de la construcción; es completamente libre e ilimitado – es mágico. Un encantamiento se apodera de la piel de la fachada y en cualquier momento puede surgir algo nuevo. La fachada mediática ofrece la oportunidad de transmitir calidad emocional a los exteriores de los edificios. Quizás guarda relación con ello también nuestro vago anhelo de que el entorno edificado, en lugar de orientarse únicamente a lo funcional y lo racional, se convierta en un ámbito que consiga conmovernos más profundamente en los complejos pliegues de nuestro espíritu. La evolución arquitectónica de los últimos tiempos refleja una creciente necesidad de complejidad. Tal vez necesitamos espacios vitales que se acompasen de modo más apropiado y armónico a nuestras emociones y sensaciones íntimas. ¿Buscamos acaso con ello una armonía entre nuestros mundos interior y exterior? En nuestra naturaleza humana hay un gran desgarramiento interno: por un lado, necesitamos directrices claras a las que poder aferrarnos y, por otro, oponemos resistencia a esas disposiciones si creemos que no se corresponden con el mundo interior que cada uno de nosotros sentimos. Por esta razón, todo lo que queda abierto y no se define con exactitud, todo lo que esconde algo inconcebible resulta increíblemente atractivo. Por ello, a todos nos cautiva lo que está envuelto de cierta magia. Toda experiencia con lo misterioso alberga la ilusión de que las circunstancias vitales propias no estén clausuradas, de que aún haya otras posibilidades.

Visión

Sin embargo, la situación actual de nuestro entorno edificado muy pocas veces puede permitirse desplegar dicha magia. Las presiones económicas son demasiado fuertes. Nuestras ciudades son por regla general una secuencia relativamente aleatoria de edificaciones, que apenas son capaces de producir algo misterioso con su interacción. En estos casos, una fachada mediática constituye una ampliación fundamental de posibilidades: es capaz de romper el aislamiento constructivo de una fachada y establecer de ese modo una relación dinámica entre otras fachadas en el contexto urbano. Para ello sólo se precisa ajustar entre sí los contenidos de la escenificación de los distintos edificios con criterios mediáticos. De tal forma, el espacio urbano puede recobrar su cualidad de contexto sensorial perceptible. Por ello, mi propuesta es que las ciudades que cuenten con varias fachadas mediáticas elaboren y apliquen unas normas reguladoras de los contenidos mostrados. Sólo de ese modo puede edificarse una cultura de la escenificación del espacio urbano íntegra y acabarse asimismo con el uso inadecuado de las superficies mediáticas (por ejemplo, con publicidad agresiva).

Cambio de paradigmas

La condición de partida para una normativa reguladora de tales características es el examen detenido de los fenómenos de la percepción. El nuevo medio "fachada mediática" transforma la actitud estática de la arquitectura en un espejo del estado anímico momentáneo de su entorno social. Lo que se muestra en una piel mediática documenta el interés de los empresarios o usuarios por revalorizar la arquitectura de su edificio y mostrarse así hacia fuera. La mentalidad de la escenificación puede ser muy variada: desde una composición luminosa dinámica hasta una proyección de vídeo. En los casos de fachadas mediáticas con proyecciones de vídeo, se ha generalizado la sospecha de que esas fachadas pueden desembocar automáticamente en torrentes descontrolados de imágenes. Ese temor se basa en la experiencia que tenemos con los medios visuales electrónicos. El potencial que representa poder exhibir en una gran superficie imágenes electrónicas induce siempre a los implicados, en un primer momento, a reproducir en la fachada los mecanismos de un monitor. Nuestras costumbres visuales están muy condicionadas por el contexto de la televisión y por ello de un monitor esperamos que nos entretenga o informe constantemente con algo nuevo. Pero un monitor suscita siempre una fijación visual. Aísla al observador; el observador cae por completo presa de la fascinación por el medio. De ese hábito resulta la expectativa de que una fachada mediática debe incluir un programa elaborado de forma semejante al de una cadena de televisión. Sin embargo, el contexto de la arquitectura mediática es distinto. El observador de una fachada mediática no está ni mucho menos aislado. Tan pronto como se encuentra en un espacio público, no puede percibir al cien por cien las imágenes electrónicas, ya que tiene que reaccionar a demasiados estímulos al mismo tiempo. Incluso un anuncio publicitario estándar, con una estructura narrativa y una duración de unos 30 segundos, resulta inapropiado en un espacio público, ya que un anuncio así trabaja en la mayoría de los casos con el efecto de un clímax. Un público que a su vez está en movimiento no le dedica la atención necesaria para llegar a ese momento. Por ese motivo, la escenificación de una fachada mediática apuesta por escalas completamente inéditas, y precisamente ahí está la posibilidad de una cultura perfilada en consonancia con los tiempos. En cada proyecto de fachada mediática tienen que determinarse de nuevo también los parámetros en cuanto a su contenido. Éstos se desarrollan en un continuo proceso de interacción entre el propietario o usuario del edificio, la ciudad y la evolución social del momento. La mediatización de nuestro entorno edificado se transforma así en la metodología de una reflexión integral, que demuestra en qué medida actuamos en sociedad. Cualquier puesta en escena de una fachada mediática que desagrade lo más mínimo puede modificarse rápidamente, a diferencia de lo que ocurre con la arquitectura. En cierto modo, este tipo de mediatización induce a una reflexión sobre nuestras competencias e interacciones sociales. Exige constantemente que tengamos una idea clara sobre nosotros mismos y que nos preguntemos cómo queremos ser, qué atmósfera urbana está más en consonancia con nosotros. La creatividad del diseño mediático puede fijar muchos principios de la cultura de la escenificación. Ahí deberíamos estar abiertos a la posibilidad de alguna sorpresa.

Cultura urbana mediática

Como base de una normativa reguladora se pueden fijar diversos factores de creación mediática, por ejemplo el ritmo del cambio de imágenes, un canon cromático determinado o aspectos de contenido. O surge una dramaturgia exacta de cómo se quiere percibir una ciudad desde fuera hacia dentro, de modo que en el centro de las ciudades y en los accesos a las mismas se puedan mostrar contenidos distintos. Estos ejemplos, con toda seguridad insólitos en el mundo de la arquitectura, muestran que hay que pensar en muchas direcciones. La elaboración de una normativa reguladora puede llegar a tener importancia económica para una ciudad o región determinada - especialmente en el contexto global -. ¿Qué ciudad puede prescindir hoy de un marketing individualizado? Para poder ser tomada en cuenta en el circuito económico del capital y de los inversores, debe despuntar. Con ayuda de una cultura urbana mediatizada pueden subrayarse perfiles específicos que transmiten la imagen económica que un lugar tiene de sí mismo. En este caso, la inversión en la dinámica de los medios electrónicos es muy ventajosa a largo plazo. Una ciudad como Colonia podría emprender, por ejemplo, una mediatización controlada con criterio teatral de sus puentes, para de ese modo cimentar sus pretensiones de ciudad mediática y artística. Al mismo tiempo, se estaría escenificando la amable naturaleza renana, consiguiendo así enraizar la cultura regional en la imagen urbana. La iniciación de fachadas mediatizadas electrónicamente resulta estimulante sólo por el mero hecho de que se pone de manifiesto la pertenencia a un juego global: se es innovador y moderno o, dicho de otro modo, "the medium is the message". La concepción de los contenidos de tales fachadas también tiene que documentar siempre, como es lógico, los intereses de los usuarios del edificio concreto o del inversor. El modo y la forma del diseño mediático pueden someterse, pese a todo, al metaorden de una normativa reguladora urbana. No ocurre de otro modo en las realizaciones arquitectónicas y urbanísticas.

Perspectivas

Las posibilidades de una arquitectura mediatizada –una mediatectura– para nuestro entorno edificado están en nuestras manos. Todo depende de lo que todos los implicados hagan de ella: se trata de un complejo proceso social. La mediatectura forja vínculos entre las personas y su entorno edificado. El anhelo de terruño y cultura regional se hace cada vez más patente en el juego global de las fuerzas económicas, y puede ser asumido por la mediatectura. Para ello, nosotros los mediatectos no reaccionaremos sólo a los requisitos directos de cada proceso constructivo; sincronizaremos y armonizaremos las necesidades comunicativas de los usuarios del edificio con la situación cultural del lugar concreto del proyecto. Se trata de poner de relieve la identidad de un lugar. Ello no va a cambiar el papel del arquitecto. Él seguirá aportando la idea fundamental de una obra. El mediatecto se ofrece como compañero del arquitecto para asumir y llevar adelante los contenidos de sus ideas arquitectónicas en la sincronización general de la orientación mediática. Así puede surgir un entorno edificado en consonancia con un mundo vital muy influido por internet y otros medios de comunicación.

La facciata mediatica come elemento della cultura urbana di Christoph Kronhagel

In tutto il mondo si assiste oggi a un'aumentata esigenza di medializzare elettronicamente le opere architettoniche; cerchiamo di seguito di analizzarne le ragioni. Osserviamo come influisce sull'ambiente edificato una medializzazione elettronica: una costruzione in sé del tutto statica, come quella di una facciata, si mette d'un tratto in movimento. Questo movimento non ha nulla a che fare con la funzionalità della costruzione, ma è del tutto libero e privo di limitazioni – di più, ha qualcosa di magico. Un incantesimo si è posato sulla superficie esterna dell'edificio e in ogni momento può accadere qualcosa di nuovo. La facciata mediatica offre dunque la possibilità di riempire con le emozioni il nostro spazio vitale. Forse c'è anche un certo desiderio di non vivere in un mondo di edifici orientati esclusivamente in senso funzionale-razionalistico, ma di trasformarli in luoghi che riescano a toccarci molto più in profondità, negli strati più complessi dell'anima. Lo sviluppo architettonico degli ultimi anni rispecchia una crescente tendenza verso una sempre maggiore complessità. Probabilmente c'è bisogno di spazi vitali che accompagnino in modo adeguato e armonioso le nostre tensioni e sensazioni interiori. O forse siamo in cerca di un rapporto autentico tra il nostro mondo interiore e il mondo esterno? Nella natura umana è insita una lacerazione epocale: da una parte abbiamo la necessità di punti di riferimento chiari, sui quali poter fare affidamento, e allo stesso tempo ci opponiamo a queste regole, se non le percepiamo più come autentiche e rispondenti al mondo interiore nella sua continua mutevolezza. Per questo siamo affascinati da tutto ciò che rimane aperto e non definito con esattezza, ciò che nasconde in sé qualcosa di intangibile; pertanto amiamo tutto ciò che risplende di una certa magia. Ogni esperienza di mistero ha in sé la speranza che determinate condizioni di vita non siano concluse in se stesse, ma che offrano ancora nuove possibilità.

Visione

La situazione contemporanea del nostro ambiente edificato si presta tuttavia di rado a dispiegare tale senso di magia. In questo senso, le pressioni economiche sono troppo forti. Le città sono piuttosto una sequenza relativamente casuale di corpi di edifici, che nella loro interazione lasciano poco spazio al mistero. È proprio qui che la facciata mediatica si pone come elemento fondamentale di ampliamento delle prospettive: è in grado di infrangere la chiusura costruttiva di una facciata, di modo che in un contesto urbanistico le facciate entrino in rapporto dinamico l'una con l'altra. A questo scopo è necessario solo adeguare tra loro i contenuti della messa in scena dei diversi edifici dal punto di vista mediatico e creativo, cosicché lo spazio urbano riesca a recuperare nuovamente di una relazione che possa essere percepita in maniera sensoriale. Per questo propongo che le città con diverse facciate mediatiche elaborino e mettano in pratica una sorta di decalogo creativo per i contenuti da mettere in scena. In questo modo diventa possibile costruire una cultura della messa in scena complessiva dello spazio urbano e con essa anche limitare l'abuso della superficie medializzata (per esempio con una pubblicità troppo aggressiva).

Cambiamenti di paradigmi

Per poter stilare tale decalogo creativo, è necessario prima occuparsi a fondo dei fenomeni di percezione. Il nuovo medium "facciata mediatica" trasforma il comportamento statico di un'opera architettonica in uno specchio degli eventi che si svolgono in quel momento nell'ambiente sociale in cui si trova. Ciò che viene messo in scena su una superficie medializzata documenta l'interesse, da parte di chi la gestisce o del fruitore, a valorizzare l'architettura di quell'edificio e a dimostrarlo all'esterno. La mentalità a monte di una messa in scena può essere quanto mai sfaccettata: si può andare da un semplice gioco di luci dinamico fino alla messa in scena di video e film. Nel caso di facciate mediatiche che mettono in scena videofilmati è molto diffusa l'idea che tali superfici medializzate diventino automaticamente dei megaschermi dove passano film e immagini in modo incontrollato. È un timore che trova fondamento nelle passate esperienze con i mezzi di comunicazione visiva. La possibilità di far passare elettronicamente delle immagini su una vasta superficie induce gli interessati a riprodurre sulla facciata innanzitutto i meccanismi di un monitor. Le nostre abitudini visive sono fortemente condizionate dal contesto televisivo e tendiamo dunque ad aspettarci che da un monitor provenga continuamente qualcosa di nuovo, sia sotto forma di intrattenimento che di informazione. Viceversa, un monitor provoca sempre una fissazione dello sguardo. Esso isola l'osservatore, il quale viene catturato completamente dalla malìa del mezzo. Da questa abitudine scaturisce il presupposto che una facciata mediatica debba riprodurre un programma redazionale, esattamente come un canale TV. Ma questo nesso, nel caso di un'architettura medializzata, non esiste: chi osserva una facciata mediatica è tutt'altro che isolato. Fino a che questi si trova in uno spazio pubblico, non sperimenta una percezione totale delle immagini elettroniche, perché si trova a dover reagire nello stesso tempo a diversi stimoli. Già una normale clip pubblicitaria con una struttura narrativa di circa 30 secondi non funziona più in uno spazio pubblico, in quanto generalmente si risolve con un finale.

L'attenzione necessaria a seguire il filo del discorso non può provenire da un pubblico che a sua volta è in movimento. La messa in scena di una facciata mediatica crea una dimensione totalmente nuova, e sta esattamente qui la possibilità di dare vita a una nuova cultura della città, al passo con i tempi. Per ogni nuovo progetto di facciata mediatica è necessario determinare in modo personalizzato i parametri dei contenuti. Essi si evolvono in un costante processo d'interazione tra proprietario o utente dell'edificio, città e sviluppi sociali in corso. La medializzazione del nostro mondo edificato si trasforma quindi in una metodica per una riflessione integrata, in grado di spiegare in quale forma dovremmo agire collettivamente. La messa in scena di una facciata mediatica che crei disappunto o malumore in qualsivoglia forma e modalità può essere modificata in tempo reale, contrariamente all'architettura. In un certo modo, questo tipo di medializzazione provoca una riflessione sulle nostre competenze sociali e sulle nostre interazioni collettive. Ci sfida continuamente a essere chiari con noi stessi e a porci la domanda: come vogliamo essere? Qual è l'atmosfera urbana più adatta a noi? La creatività del design mediatico può produrre diversi principi della cultura della medializzazione – stiamo a vedere cosa siamo in grado di fare.

Cultura urbana mediatica

Come fondamento di quel decalogo creativo di cui parlavamo più sopra, possiamo definire diversi fattori della creatività mediatica, ad esempio il ritmo con cui si susseguono le immagini, un preciso canone della tonalità cromatica o aspetti relativi ai contenuti. Oppure ne deriva una vera e propria drammaturgia su come si desidera percepire una città dall'esterno verso l'interno, cosicché in centro vengono rappresentati contenuti diversi da quelli dei percorsi d'accesso. Tali esempi, certamente inconsueti per il settore dell'architettura, mostrano che è necessario pensare in più direzioni. La messa a punto di un decalogo creativo mediatico potrà acquisire un significato economico a seconda della città o della regione in cui viene messo in pratica; e questo vale, a maggior ragione, in un contesto globale. Quale città riesce oggi a sopravvivere senza un marketing personalizzato? Per distinguersi nella ristretta cerchia economica del capitale e degli investitori, è necessario farsi notare. Attraverso una cultura medializzata della città è possibile mettere in risalto profili particolari, in grado di comunicare l'autoconsapevolezza economica di un luogo o di una zona precisa. A questo riguardo, l'investimento a lungo termine nella dinamica dei mezzi di comunicazione elettronici è molto efficiente. Una città come Colonia, per esempio, potrebbe medializzare in modo drammaturgico e controllato i suoi ponti, rafforzando così la sua immagine di città d'arte e dei media. Allo stesso tempo verrebbe messa in scena la giovialità del carattere renano, agganciando così la cultura regionale all'immagine della città. La promozione di facciate medializzate ha già di per sé il proprio fascino, perché con essa si dimostra che si sta partecipando a un gioco globale: essere innovativi e moderni o, in altre parole, comunicare che "The medium is the message". L'organizzazione dei contenuti di questo tipo di facciate deve anche documentare, naturalmente, gli interessi comunicativi del fruitore dell'edificio, oppure dell'investitore. Il tipo e la modalità del design mediatico possono tuttavia essere soggetti al metaordinamento di un decalogo creativo della città, non diversamente da quanto accade nel caso dell'architettura e dell'urbanistica.

Previsione

Le possibilità di un'architettura medializzata – o di una mediatettura – per il nostro ambiente edificato sono racchiuse in noi stessi. Dipende da quanto faranno tutte le parti interessate, e si tratta comunque di un processo sociale complesso. La mediatettura crea collegamenti tra le persone e il loro ambiente edificato. Il desiderio di riconoscersi in una patria e in una cultura regionale acquista sempre maggior significato nel gioco globale delle forze economiche e può essere restituito attraverso la mediatettura. Noi "architetti mediatici" non reagiremo perciò solo alle richieste dirette del processo costruttivo di turno. Dovremo conciliare e armonizzare le necessità comunicative del fruitore dell'edificio con le varie situazioni culturali del luogo dove verrà realizzato il progetto; si tratta di far risaltare da tutto ciò l'identità del luogo. Il ruolo dell' architetto, in questo senso, non sarà diverso. Come è sempre avvenuto, egli mette insieme alcune idee di fondo e un edificio. Si tratta però di una nuova figura di professionista dei nuovi media, che si propone come partner dell'architetto, allo scopo di recepirne le idee e amplificarle dal punto di vista dei contenuti e dell'armonizzazione complessiva dell'allestimento mediatico. In questo modo si potrà dare vita a un ambiente edificato che corrisponde a un *Lebenswelt*, mondo quotidiano, influenzato in larga misura da Internet e da altri mezzi di comunicazione.

© 2006 daab
cologne london new york

published and distributed worldwide by
daab gmbh
friesenstr. 50
d - 50670 köln

p +49 - 221 - 94 10 740
f +49 - 221 - 94 10 741

mail@daab-online.com
www.daab-online.com

publisher ralf daab
rdaab@daab-online.com

creative director feyyaz
mail@feyyaz.com

layout marc van der ploeg
mail@vdp-design.de

editorial project © 2006 by ag4 mediatecture company®
contact@ag4.de
www.ag4.de / www.mediafacade.com

text by ag4 mediatecture company®
christoph kronhagel, ralf müller, steffen tabel and klaus teltenkoetter

all renderings and animations by ag4 mediatecture company®
marc everz, david seabra and klaus teltenkoetter

renderings
"Spirit" and "Time" by david seabra and deepartmend sascha selent
"Urban" by deepartmend sascha selent

dvd authoring by ag4 mediatecture company®
klaus teltenkoetter and atelier für mediengestaltung, cologne

photos
arne hofmann, lutz korn, gardin&mazzoli, stefan schilling, hans joerg uhl

english translation ingo wagener
french translation valérie schawe
italian translation paola vitale
spanish translation virtudes mayayo
translations and copy editing by durante & zoratti, cologne

printed in germany

isbn-10   3 - 937718 - 97 - 4
isbn-13   978 - 3 - 937718 - 97 - 2